Exercise Book

for

The Ready Reference Handbook

Writing, Revising, Editing

Jack Dodds
William Rainey Harper College

Allyn and Bacon
Boston · London · Toronto · Sydney · Tokyo · Singapore

A Viacom Company
160 Gould Street
Needham Heights, Massachusetts 02194

Internet: www.abacon.com
America Online: keyword: College Online

ISBN 0-205-26696-7

Printed in the United States of America

10 9 8 7 6 5 4 3 02 01 00 99 98 97

Contents

Choosing Words

Editing English as a Second Language

Punctuating

Notes for Instructors and Students

A Note for Instructors

The exercises in this booklet are linked to sections in *The Ready Reference Handbook* identified in the instructions preceding each exercise. Students should, of course, read the appropriate section before beginning an exercise. You may use these exercises as homework, as in-class practice, as individual tutorials to prepare students to edit their own writing, or for quizzes and exams. You may photocopy this booklet for students or ask them to purchase their own copies.

Most exercises consist of several lettered items followed by three to fifteen numbered items. Answers to lettered items appear at the back of this booklet so that students can check their understanding as they begin a particular exercise. In addition, exercises are illustrated with an example showing students how to perform the required editing. The majority of exercises have been double spaced so that students may add, delete, and rearrange as they would if editing their own writing. A few require filling in blanks or recopying to produce a thorough revision.

You may assign all the items in an exercise or, for review purposes, only a few (such as odd-numbered items). If you wish students to work independently, you may photocopy the complete answer key that accompanies this booklet. A few items for which many right answers are possible have not been included in this key.

A Note for Students

Writers, like painters and pianists, learn their art in part by practicing, whether sketching perspectives, playing musical scales, or writing exercises in a booklet like this. By doing these exercises you'll train your eye and ear to recognize well-crafted sentences, you'll learn how to create them yourself, and you'll acquire a precise vocabulary to help you describe your writing and talk about it with others.

These exercises are linked to sections in *The Ready Reference Handbook* identified in the instructions preceding each exercise. Read the appropriate section before beginning an exercise. You'll see that most exercises consist of several lettered items followed by three to fifteen numbered items. Answers to lettered items appear at the back of this booklet so that you can check your understanding as you begin a particular exercise. (A few items for which many right answers are possible have not been included in this key.) In addition, many exercises are illustrated with an example showing you how to perform the required editing. And the majority have been double spaced so that you may add, delete, and rearrange as you would if editing your own writing. A few require filling in blanks or recopying to produce a thorough revision.

You may do these exercises as homework, as in-class practice, as individual practice to prepare yourself to edit your own writing, or as quizzes and exams. You may be assigned to do all the items in an exercise or, for review purposes, only a few (such as odd-numbered items).

Composing

Exercise 1--Creating Your Voice (Persona)

For each of the following situations write a brief memo that could be sent as an e-mail message. (Your instructor may tell you to choose one or two of the options.) In each case, the voice you create in your writing--your persona--will be crucial to your success. To learn more about voice, see 1d in *The Ready Reference Handbook.*

1. You are an enthusiastic member of Wild Forever, a wildlife preservation organization, which meets once a year in Hawaii. Next weekend is the annual meeting, and you've just learned that the Wild Forever Foundation has selected you to receive an all-expenses paid trip to that meeting. You must decide immediately whether you can attend; if you can't the prize will be given to someone else. What good fortune! What a trip! You're excited about spending a long weekend in the company of your fellow wildlife supporters. What's more, you work part time, go to school full time, and haven't had a day off the whole term. The weather outside is awful. You could use a long weekend in the sun.

   There's just one problem. You're taking a course this term from the fearsome Dr. Kharbide, one of your school's most difficult instructors but also one of the best. He has shown an interest in your work, and you're concerned that if you take this trip and miss his class, you'll lose whatever regard he has for you. More important, you're doing well in his class, and you must continue to do well--at least a B--to keep your scholarship. You know he will not look kindly on what he will consider a frivolous absence from his class.

   You stop by his office to discuss your dilemma with him, but he is nowhere to be found. You try calling him, but he isn't in and has no answering machine or voice mail. You can delay no longer. The Wild Forever Foundation needs to know whether you'll accept their award. You've decided to take the trip and miss Dr. Kharbide's class, but you can't just disappear. You decide to write him a message, informing him of your decision and attempting to remain in his good graces. You'll send it to him as e-mail. Write that message. By the way, you are a scrupulously honest person who never lies.

2. The Wild Forever Foundation has indicated that it will also pay all expenses for one guest to accompany you to the Hawaii meeting. You decide immediately who this person will be, another member of Dr. Kharbide's class. The problem is that this person works harder than you, is more concerned about grades, and more careful not to offend a prickly, challenging instructor like Dr. Kharbide. As much as your friend will want to accompany you on your trip, he or she will have to be persuaded to do what may at first seem irresponsible. Write an e-mail message in which you invite your friend and persuade him or her that taking this trip is the right thing to do. Again, you would never lie.

3. You have another acquaintance from Dr. Kharbide's class by the name of Leach, also a member of Wild Forever, who has just learned that you have been selected for the all-expenses-paid trip to Hawaii and who knows that you may take a guest. Leach has written you an e-mail message almost begging to be chosen as your guest. This person is not a friend and never will be, is not a pleasant person, and would make a poor companion for a trip to Hawaii. Nevertheless, Leach is a human being and doesn't deserve to be insulted or hurt. Write a considerate, tactful an e-mail message refusing Leach's request to accompany you. Of course, you would never lie.

Exercise 2--Writing Thesis Statements

Write a brief thesis statement (one to three sentences) for each of the following topics that could be the main point or message for a complete essay. Begin with the formula "My point is that . . . What I mean to say is that . . ." Then, when you're certain each thesis says what you want to say, write a final draft *without* the formula. To learn to write thesis statements, see 1e.

1. Write a thesis about what you believe to be the benefits of a college education. Example:

   My point is that a college education does more than prepare students for a career. What I mean to say is that college provides students with the experiences and knowledge that will make them interesting, complex persons and more effective citizens.

2. Write a thesis about the value of an important experience you've had.

3. Evaluate a book you've read or a movie you've seen recently.

4. Write a thesis proposing the solution to a social or environmental problem.

5. Write a thesis about a topic from the list at the back of this booklet, p. 138.

Exercise 3--Drawing Conclusions and Writing a Thesis

Following are a number of facts about Christmas. Study them carefully and decide what you can conclude about this holiday based solely on these facts. Write out your conclusion as a thesis statement that could be the main point or message for a complete essay about Christmas. Begin with the formula "My point is that . . . What I mean to say is that . . ." Then, when you're certain your thesis says what you want to say, write a final draft *without* the formula. To learn to write thesis statements, see 1e in *The Ready Reference Handbook.*

Each US adult spends an average of two days per year on Christmas activities, an investment of nearly one million person-years per season.

According to the US forest service, 33 million Christmas trees are consumed each year. Growing them imposes an artificially short rotation period on millions of acres of forest land. Disposing of them places a heavy burden on landfill sites and recycling facilities.

Christians did not observe Christmas until the fifth century. The Puritans refused to celebrate it.

In the six weeks between Thanksgiving and New Year's Day, Americans consume nearly $20 billion worth of alcohol and 2.1 billion pounds of turkey. Christmas is one of the greatest contributors to obesity. The average American consumes more than 3,500 calories at Christmas Day dinner alone.

Each year about fifteen percent of all Christmas purchases are returned.

According to Dr. Quita Mullen, Boston psychiatrist, women exhaust themselves trying to meet the demands of full-time jobs and, simultaneously, the traditional expectations of what the holidays are supposed to be like.

Christmas now accounts for sixty percent of the US's annual $17 billion expenditure on toys and video games.

Police, psychiatrists, and hospitals report a dramatic rise in alcoholic "slips," drug overdoses, domestic quarrels, hotline calls, and emergency medical calls during the Christmas season.

Airlines, mail delivery systems, stores, banks, warehouses, telephone systems, roads, and parking lots must be built larger than they would otherwise be solely to handle Christmas activities.

According to the US Commerce Department, Americans spend $40-50 billion annually on what they report as unnecessary or unjustified gifts.

There are 350 Teenage Mutant Ninja Turtle products.

Americans save less than five percent of their annual income.

December is the peak month in the US for robberies and the second highest for auto theft.

Each year there are 33 deaths and 148,000 emergency room admissions due to hazardous toys, plus 1.2 million toy recalls.

Deaths caused by books: 0.

Christmas is the season of most household fires. The Washington, DC, fire department reports fire calls forty percent above the monthly average; New York City reported 2,800 residential fires during Christmas 1989, compared with a 2,000-per-month average.

December 21 and 22 are peak dates for air travel, with nearly two million Americans per day passing through airports. Twenty-three million travel from December 19-January 4. During this period American weather is often at its worst and airlines charge their highest fares.

The US now spends nearly as much on video games ($4 billion), activity figures like World Wrestlers ($500 million), and dolls like Barbie ($1.1 billion) as on all retail book sales ($6.6 billion).

December is the peak month for drunk driving and DUI arrests (nearly two million).

Almost one-quarter of Christmas sales are financed by credit cards or charge accounts. January is the peak month for credit card delinquencies.

According to the Humane Society, 4 million foxes and minks will be killed to provide Christmas furs. To serve Christmas dinners we slaughter 22 million turkeys, 2 million pigs, 2-3 million cattle, and a large share of the 6 billion chickens the US consumes each year.

December is the peak month for motor vehicle accidents, nearly half a million each year, compared to a monthly average of just over 350,000.

(Data compiled by James S. Henry, *The New Republic,* December 31, 1990.)

Exercise 4--Organizing Information (Outlining)

Write an outline in which you organize the information in the preceding exercise (Exercise 3) into a logical pattern. If you have written a thesis statement for Exercise 3, base your outline upon it. (Your outline does not have to include all the information listed here.) Group the information into appropriate categories, and identify these categories with major subject headings (section *I, II, III,* and so forth). Then list the appropriate information beneath each heading (*I. A., B., C.; II. A., B., C,* and so forth) or create subheadings, each with its own list of appropriate information (*I. A. 1., 2.; I. B. 1.,* 2., and so forth). To learn to write an outline, see 2c in *The Ready Reference Handbook.*

Exercise 5--Writing Unified, Well-Developed Paragraphs

Choose three topics from the list at the end of this booklet (p. 138) and for each write a unified, well-developed paragraph. Write a topic sentence to focus your paragraph, and choose an appropriate method of paragraph development to support your topic sentence. To learn to write topic sentences, see 5a in *The Ready Reference Handbook.* To choose methods of paragraph development, see 6b1-6b10.

Identifying Grammar

Exercise 6--Identifying Parts of Speech: Nouns

Underline nouns, noun/adjectives (nouns functioning as adjectives), and verbal nouns (verbs functioning as nouns) in the following sentences. To learn about nouns, see 8a in *The Ready Reference Handbook*. Answers to lettered items appear in the back of this booklet. Example:

A <u>lover's</u> <u>eyes</u> will gaze an <u>eagle</u> blind.

--William Shakespeare

a. Honey catches more flies than vinegar.

--Italian proverb

b. In Wildness is the preservation of the world.

--Henry David Thoreau

c. Convictions are more dangerous enemies of truth than lies.

--Friedrich Nietzsche

d. The cruelest lies are often told in silence.

--Robert Louis Stevenson

e. Courage is resistance to fear, mastery of fear--not absence of fear.

--Mark Twain

1. Quarrels would not last long if the fault were only on one side.

--La Rochefoucauld

2. Woman's virtue is man's greatest invention.

--Cornelia Otis Skinner

3. The wind and the waves are always on the side of the ablest navigators.

--Edward Gibbon

4. Hypocrisy is the homage vice pays to virtue.

--La Rochefoucauld

5. The trouble with the profit system has always been that it was highly unprofitable to most people.

--E. B. White

Exercise 7--Identifying Parts of Speech: Pronouns

Underline pronouns and pronoun/adjectives (pronouns functioning as adjectives) in the following sentences. To learn about pronouns, see 8b in *The Ready Reference Handbook*. Answers to lettered items appear in the back of this booklet. Example:

The hour which gives us life begins to take it away.

--Seneca

a. The only thing we have to fear is fear itself.

--Franklin Delano Roosevelt

b. We often forgive those who bore us but never those whom we bore.

La Rochefoucauld

c. If you can't say something good about someone, sit right here by me.

--Alice Roosevelt Longworth

d. Mishaps are like knives, that either serve us or cut us, as we grasp them by the blade or the handle.

--James Russell Lowell

e. Experience is the name everyone gives to their mistakes.

--Oscar Wilde

1. There's only one corner of the universe you can be certain of improving, and that's your own self.

--Aldous Huxley

2. When people are free to do as they please, they usually imitate each other.

--Eric Hoffer

3. Those who deny freedom to others deserve it not for themselves.

--Abraham Lincoln

4. The limits of my language mean the limits of my world.

--Ludwig Wittgenstein

5. Most of our misfortunes are more supportable than the comments of our friends upon them.

--Charles Caleb Colton

Exercise 8--Identifying Parts of Speech: Verbs

Underline verbs in the following sentences, including helping verbs and particles (the preposition-like words in two-word verbs). To learn about verbs, see 8c in *The Ready Reference Handbook.* Answers to lettered items appear in the back of this booklet. Example:

> **Conscience is the inner voice which warns us that someone may be looking.**

--H. L. Mencken

a. I never forget a face, but I'll make an exception in your case.

--Groucho Marx

b. Life shrinks or expands in proportion to one's courage.

--Anaïs Nin

c. The world oftener applauds the appearance of virtue than it does virtue itself.

--La Rochefoucauld

d. Nothing can be created out of nothing.

--Lucretius

e. The world can only be grasped by action, not by contemplation.

--Jacob Bronowski

1. Our deeds determine us, as much as we determine our deeds.

--George Eliot

2. A great many people think they are thinking when they are merely rearranging their prejudices.

--William James

3. Nothing great was ever achieved without enthusiasm.

--Ralph Waldo Emerson

4. Everything that can be said can be said clearly.

--Ludwig Wittgenstein

5. We always like our admirers; we do not always like those we admire.

--La Rochefoucauld

Exercise 9--Identifying Parts of Speech: Adjectives and Adverbs

Underline the adjectives and circle the adverbs in the following sentences. Treat articles, adjective-like pronouns, and adjective-like verbs as adjectives. To learn about adjectives and adverbs, see 8d and e in *The Ready Reference Handbook.* Answers to lettered items appear in the back of this booklet. Example:

> **A little sincerity is a dangerous thing, and a great deal of it is absolutely fatal.**

--Oscar Wilde

a. A great fortune is a great slavery.

--Seneca

b. Even a blind pig occasionally picks up an acorn.

--American proverb

c. Poverty and isolation produce impoverished and isolated minds.

--William Gass

d. Old age isn't so bad when you consider the alternatives.

--Maurice Chevalier

e. No one ever suddenly became depraved.

--Juvenal

1. It is better to travel hopefully than to arrive.

--Robert Louis Stevenson

2. Books are the quietest and most constant of friends; they are the most accessible and wisest of counsellors, and the most patient of teachers.

--Charles W. Eliot

3. Many people live in ugly wastelands, but in the absence of imaginative standards, most of them do not even know it.

--C. Wright Mills

4. It was a wise man who said that there is no greater inequality than the equal treatment of unequals.

--Felix Frankfurter

5. Power tends to corrupt, and absolute power corrupts absolutely.

--Lord Acton

Exercise 10--Identifying Sentence Parts: Subjects and Verbs

In the following sentences, underline the complete subjects; double underline the complete verbs that describe the action or state of being of the subjects. If the subject is an understood *you,* insert it at the appropriate place. To learn about subjects, see 9a in *The Ready Reference Handbook.* To learn about verbs, see 8c. Answers to lettered items appear in the back of this booklet. Example:

An injury is much sooner forgotten than an insult.

--Lord Chesterton

a. You can tell the ideals of a nation by its advertisements.

--Norman Douglas

b. Hitch your wagon to a star.

--Ralph Waldo Emerson

c. Love and a cough cannot be hid.

--George Herbert

d. Dreaming permits each and every one of us to be quietly and safely insane every night of our lives.

--Charles Fisher

e. There is always an easy solution to every human problem--neat, plausible, and wrong.

--H. L. Mencken

1. Love and scandal are the best sweeteners of tea.

--Henry Fielding

2. In a consumer society there are inevitably two kinds of slaves: the prisoners of addiction and the prisoners of envy.

--Ivan Illich

3. Love art. Of all lies, it is the least untrue.

--Gustave Flaubert

4. I've worked myself up from nothing to a state of extreme poverty.

--Groucho Marx

5. A little rebellion, now and then, is a good thing, and as necessary in the political world as storms in the physical.

--Thomas Jefferson

Exercise 11--Identifying Sentence Parts: Prepositional Phrases

Underline the prepositional phrases in the following sentences. Then describe their sentence functions as subjects, complements, direct objects, adjective-like modifiers, or adverb-like modifiers. To learn about prepositional phrases, see 10a1 in *The Ready Reference Handbook.* Answers to lettered items appear in the back of this booklet. Example:

Adverb phrase modifying "bury" *Adjective phrase modifying "order"*
In peace sons bury fathers, but war violates the order of nature, and fathers bury sons.

--Herodotus

a. Old age is the verdict of life.

--Amelia Barr

b. A woman without a man is like a fish without a bicycle.

--Gloria Steinem

c. The cruelest lies are often told in silence.

--Robert Louis Stevenson

d. Literature is the art of writing something that will be read twice; journalism what will be grasped at once.

--Cyril Connolly

e. The secret source of Humor itself is not joy but sorrow. There is no humor in heaven.

--Mark Twain

1. Everything is funny as long as it is happening to somebody else.

--Will Rogers

2. From the sublime to the ridiculous is but a step.

--La Bruyère

3. The bitterest tears shed over graves are for words left unsaid and deeds left undone.

--Harriet Beecher Stowe

4. In matters of grave importance, style, not sincerity, is the vital thing.

--Oscar Wilde

5. A foolish consistency is the hobgoblin of little minds, adored by little statesmen and philosophers and divines.

--Ralph Waldo Emerson

Exercise 12--Identifying Sentence Parts: Verbals and Verbal Phrases

Underline the verbals and verbal phrases in the following sentences. Identify them as gerunds, participles, or infinitives and describe their sentence functions as subjects, direct objects, complements, objects of prepositions, or modifiers. To learn about verbals and verbal phrases, see 8c8 and 10a2 in *The Ready Reference Handbook*. Answers to lettered items appear in the back of this booklet. Example:

> **Words are, of course, the most powerful drug used by mankind.** *Participial phrase modifying "drug."*
>
> --Rudyard Kipling

a. Barking dogs never bite.

--English proverb

b. Lazy people are always wanting to do something.

--Marquis De Vauvenargues

c. Concealing a disease is no way to cure it.

--Ethiopian proverb

d. Arguments are to be avoided; they are always vulgar and often convincing.

--Oscar Wilde

e. The first rule of intelligent tinkering is to save all the parts.

--Paul Ehrlich

1. Stolen waters are sweet, and bread eaten in secret is pleasant.

--The Bible

2. Who dares to teach must never cease to learn.

--John Cotton Dana

3. The reward of a thing well done is to have done it.

--Ralph Waldo Emerson

4. To be forewarned is to be forearmed.

--Latin proverb

5. All rising to a great place is by a winding stair.

--Francis Bacon

Exercise 13--Identifying Sentence Parts: Dependent Clauses

Underline the dependent (also called "subordinate") clauses in the following sentences. Identify each clause as a noun, adjective, or adverb and describe its sentence function as a subject, object, complement, or modifier. To learn about dependent clauses, see 10b in *The Ready Reference Handbook.* Answers to lettered items appear in the back of this booklet. Example:

Adverb clause modifying "ceases"

Love ceases to be a pleasure when it ceases to be a secret.

--Aphra Behn

a. Beware of all enterprises that require new clothes.

--Henry David Thoreau

b. Youth is easily deceived because it is quick to hope.

--Aristotle

c. In violence, we forget who we are.

--Mary McCarthy

d. The golden rule is that there are no golden rules.

--George Bernard Shaw

e. There is nothing new except what has been forgotten.

--Mademoiselle Bertin

1. Those who do not feel pain seldom think that it is felt.

--Samuel Johnson

2. Where there is no vision, the people perish.

--Bible

3. What makes the vanity of others insupportable is that it wounds our own.

--La Rochefoucauld

4. There are many who dare not kill themselves for fear of what the neighbors will say.

--Cyril Connolly

5. A bank is a place that will lend you money if you can prove that you don't need it.

--Bob Hope

Exercise 14--Identifying Sentence Types

Identify the following sentences as simple, compound, complex, or compound-complex. Underline the dependent clauses in complex and compound-complex sentences. To learn about clauses and sentence types, see 10c in *The Ready Reference Handbook.* Answers to lettered items appear in the back of this booklet. Example:

> **If you are foolish enough to be contented, don't show it, but grumble with the rest.** *Compound-complex sentence*

--Jerome K. Jerome

a. Every generation laughs at the old fashions but follows religiously the new.

--Henry David Thoreau

b. Although the world is full of suffering, it is full also of the overcoming of it.

--Helen Keller

c. Children have never been very good at listening to their elders, but they have never failed to imitate them.

--James Baldwin

d. America is so vast that almost everything said about it is likely to be true, and the opposite is probably equally true.

--James T. Farrell

e. It's not the voting that's democracy; it's the counting.

--Tom Stoppard

1. All charming people have something to conceal, usually their total dependence on the appreciation of others.

   --Cyril Connolly

2. The only certainty is that nothing is certain.

   --Pliny the Elder

3. Competition brings out the best in products and the worst in people.

   --David Sarnoff

4. In this world there are only two tragedies. One is not getting what one wants, and the other is getting it.

   --Oscar Wilde

5. Beauty is all very well at first sight, but who ever looks at it when it has been in the house three days?

   --George Bernard Shaw

Exercise 15--Practicing Sentence Types

Study the sentences that you have identified in the preceding exercise and then write two examples of your own of simple, compound, complex, and compound-complex sentences (eight sentences total). Choose topics from the list at the end of this booklet (p. 138). To learn about sentence types, see 10c in *The Ready Reference Handbook.*

Exercise 16--Avoiding Sentence Fragments

The following correctly written examples illustrate the kinds of sentences that some writers break into fragments, word groups lacking a subject, verb, or both. To practice writing complete sentences, study these examples and write your own version of each on a separate sheet of paper. The list of topics on p. 138 will give you ideas for your writing. To learn about the parts of complete sentences, see 9a-9d in *The Ready Reference Handbook.* Example:

A sentence ending with a comma + explanatory words:

> **All charming people have something to conceal, usually their total dependence on the appreciation of others.**
>
> **--Cyril Connolly**

> *For some students, computers are a box filled with enticing distractions, such as games to while away study time and Internet pathways that lead far from the subject of the paper to be written.*

1. *A sentence ending with a comma + an explanatory word or phrase:*

   Every great mistake has a halfway moment, a split second when it can be recalled and perhaps remedied.

   --Pearl S. Buck

2. *A sentence ending with a colon or dash + an explanatory word or phrase:*

   We live, as we dream--alone.

   --Joseph Conrad

3. *A sentence ending with a phrase headed by an* -ing *or* -ed *verb:*

   Poetry is the opening and closing of a door, leaving those who look through to guess about what is seen during a moment.

   --Carl Sandburg

4. *A sentence ending with a clause headed by a relative pronoun (*who, whom, which, that):

   I always keep a supply of stimulant handy in case I see a snake--which I also keep handy.

   --W. C. Fields

5. *A sentence ending with a clause headed by a subordinating conjunction like* because, when, if since, *and so forth:*

   Youth is easily deceived because it is quick to hope.

   --Aristotle

6. *A sentence ending with a comma, colon, or dash + a list:*

   It is by the goodness of God that in our country we have those three unspeakably precious things: freedom of speech, freedom of conscience, and the prudence never to practice either of them.

   --Mark Twain

7. *A sentence ending with two word groups linked by* and, but, or, nor, yet, for, so:

   Genius is one percent inspiration and ninety-nine percent perspiration.

   --Thomas A. Edison

8. *A sentence with two verbs phrases linked by* and, but, or, nor, yet, for, so *(a compound predicate):*

   Everyone laughs at the old fashions but follows religiously the new.

   --Henry David Thoreau

9. *A sentence with two verb phrases linked by* then:

   A celebrity is a person who works hard all his life to become well known, then wears dark glasses to avoid being recognized.

   --Fred Allen

10. *A sentence ending with a prepositional phrase:*

    In the long run every government is the exact symbol of its people, with their wisdom and unwisdom.

    --Thomas Carlyle

Exercise 17--Fixing Fragments

Fix sentence fragments by connecting them to nearby sentences or by rewriting them as complete sentences. If an item is correct, write "correct" after it. To learn to identify and fix sentence fragments, see 11a and b in *The Ready Reference Handbook.* Answers to lettered items appear in the back of this booklet. Example:

My favorite vacation spot is Rock Island. ~~A~~ rugged, windswept little island located in northern Lake Michigan, near Door County, Wisconsin.

a. The causes of social status are many. The possession of money, education, relationship to political power, the accidents of birth or geography, even physical appearance.

b. Strategies in chess are determined by the designated movements of each piece. As well as the initial arrangement of the pieces on the board.

c. In most games, the winner earns the most points, but in some games, the object is to end with the fewest points. One example is darts.

d. The majority of smokers begin to smoke as teenagers. Seventy-five percent by age seventeen, eighty-nine percent by age nineteen.

e. Gena lay awake throughout the storm. Listening to the branches of the ancient crabapple scratching the side of her house.

1. Tanglewood Restaurant offers a delicious and unusual buffet. A world-wide variety of spicy dishes never tasted by most Americans.
2. Cultural assimilation occurs when immigrants adopt the culture and habits of their host country. And, in turn, add some of their customs and beliefs to the majority culture.
3. The best dish on the menu is the fiesta salad. Piled high with strips of yellow, green, and red peppers and huge chunks of charbroiled chicken.
4. The best coach I've ever had is Mrs. Jacobs. A person who can clearly explain how to do something and then show step by step how to do it.
5. Every childhood experience, whether small or large, has helped to shape the adult you've become. Your first day in school, the falls you took learning to ride a bike, the books your parents read to you as a child, your first bite of a hot dog.
6. Crispus Attucks and four others died at the "Boston Massacre." When British troops opened fire on a crowd of protestors.
7. Everyone would benefit by taking a CPR and first aid course. Not just those who work with the public.
8. During their lifetimes, smokers have higher medical bills than non-smokers, but they also die eight years sooner. Which means that they do not collect as much from Social Security or Medicare. On balance, society saves 20 to 30 cents for every pack a smoker smokes.

9. In 1840, Johnny Appleseed settled in a cabin near Mansfield, Ohio. But continued to travel hundreds of miles scattering the seeds that had given him his name.

10. Hunters pursue their sport from a variety of unrecognized motives. Such as their love of the outdoors, their quest for a kind of self sufficiency, their desire for solitude, and their pleasure in the mastery of a complex skill.

11. Now convenient shopping available to many by means of a modem and a personal computer.

12. The expressions of body language may be deliberate or unconscious. A fist waved in hostility or a shoulder drooping in resignation.

13. Most adults who try smoking soon give it up completely. Because it takes up to three years to become addicted. And because they don't feel the intense peer pressures to continue smoking until they become addicted.

14. School was out until fall, and all Barry had to worry about was getting to work on time. And deciding where to go with his friends in the evening.

15. After the Civil War, Roy Bean worked for a time as a gambler in railroad construction camps. Then went to Texas, where he had himself appointed a justice of the peace and became known as "the only law west of the Pecos."

Exercise 18--Avoiding Comma Splices

The following correctly written sentences illustrate the kinds of sentences that some writers punctuate as comma splices (two or more independent clauses linked by a comma). To practice writing correctly punctuated sentences, study these examples and write your own version of each on a separate sheet of paper. The list of topics on p. 138 will give you ideas for your writing. To learn about comma splices, see 12a and b in *The Ready Reference Handbook*. To learn about independent clauses, see 10b. Example:

Closely related independent clauses linked by a semicolon:

> **There are no classes in life for beginners; right away you are always asked to deal with what is most difficult.**
>
> **--Rainer Maria Rilke**

Ironically, anti-smoking campaigns often encourage many teenagers; they rush to do anything forbidden by those in authority.

1. *Closely related independent clauses linked by a semicolon:*

   Injustice is relatively easy to bear; what stings is justice.

   --H. L. Mencken

2. *Linked independent clauses that repeat key words:*

   Nature never deceives us; it is always we who deceive ourselves.

   --Jean-Jacques Rousseau

3. *Linked independent clauses similar in structure:*

   If you talk to God, you are praying; if God talks to you, you have schizophrenia.

   --Thomas Szasz

4. *Independent clauses linked by a colon or dash:*

   Marriage may be compared to a cage: the birds outside despair to get in, and those within despair to get out.

   --Michel De Montaigne

5. *Independent clauses linked by a semicolon + a conjunctive adverb like* however *or* therefore:

   In TV medical shows, CPR is most often performed on young accident victims who survive; however, in the real world, it is most often performed on elderly people with bad hearts who do not survive.

6. *Independent clauses linked by a semicolon + a transition like* for example *or* on the other hand:

   According to social critic H. L. Mencken, cynical governments tend to be tolerant and humane; on the other hand, those composed of fanatics are invariably oppressive.

7. *Two sentences in which a pronoun in the second refers to a noun in the first:*

   Space isn't remote at all. It's only an hour's drive away if your car could go straight upwards.

   --Fred Hoyle

8. *Linked independent clauses in which a pronoun in the second refers to a noun in the first:*

   One has to look out for engineers--they begin with sewing machines and end up with the atomic bomb.

   --Marcel Pagnol

Exercise 19--Fixing Comma Splices

Fix comma splices by repunctuating or by rewriting. If an item is correct, write "correct" after it. To learn to identify and fix comma splices, see 12a and b in *The Ready Reference Handbook.* Answers to lettered items appear in the back of this booklet. Example:

> **Colorado's mountain roads can be treacherous in winter, drivers should always carry chains and appropriate cold-weather gear.**

a. As we stood at the grave side, we had no words to share with one another, we had only our silent sorrow.

b. I was involved in a serious accident during my sophomore year of high school, ironically, it occurred on the last day of driver's ed.

c. After four hours of skiing, Michael was starving for a bratwurst, a hot dog--anything hot, spicy, and fast.

d. Women and girls have no reason to fear hemophilia, or bleeder's disease, only males are affected.

e. As the motorist knelt beside the badly injured german shepherd, all he could hear were its agonized howls.

1. Many think of television as a vast cultural wasteland, nevertheless, its potential as an educational medium is great.
2. The problems of wasteful packaging are many, they involve not only disposal but also natural resource depletion and pollution.
3. Hydroponics is sometimes referred to as tank farming, plants are grown in a liquid or a moist medium other than soil.
4. The Parisian streets were filled with tourists, they were easily identified by their fanny packs and cameras.
5. Spina bifida is a severe congenital birth defect, a child is born with an opening in the vertebral column resulting from abnormal development during early embryonic life.

6. Cheryl showed off her new car, she could tell by her brothers' expressions they were impressed.

7. As he entered the hospital room, Maurice noticed a man in the bed next to his mother, a curtain hid his face and shoulders.

8. Andrew Wyeth is a meticulously detailed painter, often his subjects seem photographed rather than painted.

9. My mother is a devoted political conservative, therefore, I end up taking liberal positions on nearly everything.

10. Fortunately, I have had excellent math teachers, otherwise, I'm not sure I would have ever learned algebra and calculus.

11. At first, Lucille couldn't find jumper cables, then when she found them, they were too short to connect one battery to the other.

12. My family members have always spent holidays and birthdays together, but my grandfather's ninetieth birthday party was special, we felt closer to one another than ever before.

13. Daniel was by no means an expert on mushrooms, he was certain, however, that the ones his brother had found were poisonous.

14. No other sports event is as thoroughly hyped as the Super Bowl, however, no event is as consistently disappointing.

15. Local politicians assume that revenues from casino gambling represent "free money," but these dollars are not free, they have been taken from other parts of the economy.

Exercise 20--Fixing Fused Sentences

Fix fused sentences by adding punctuation or by rewriting. If an item is correct, write "correct" after it. To learn to identify and fix fused sentences, see 12c in *The Ready Reference Handbook.* Answers to lettered items appear in the back of this booklet. Example:

Because
The mouth of the cave was huge ~~so~~ all of us were able to take shelter from the storm.

a. Pessimists never hope for the best they always expect the worst.

b. Losing her second job in six months didn't seem to bother Charlene she took the disappointment with her usual wisecrack and a grin.

c. When they were less than two years old, the Fox children were put in a foster home and they grew up knowing nothing of what had happened to their parents.

d. My background is similar to Irene's my mother is Spanish and came to the US just before I was born.

e. Pollution is particularly common in valleys and is densest when hot air rises and traps cool, polluted air beneath it.

1. In the oxygen cycle, oxygen is released by plants during photosynthesis and then, after being utilized by plants and animals during respiration and in burning, it combines with hydrogen and is once more available for photosynthesis.
2. To many, the Grand Canyon is nature's greatest sight but to others it is just a large hole in the ground.
3. Who knows within the next decade we may elect a woman or minority to be President of the US.
4. Gail wondered to herself why the judge was asking her to choose which parent she wanted to live with she wanted to live with both her parents in one house, like everybody else.
5. Inflation has been low for several years therefore, employers have felt justified in giving small raises to their employees.
6. To separate ourselves racially, ethnically, or religiously is as senseless as saying that someone is too tall he cannot be my friend.
7. At first glance, the Lonestar Grill looks like an old shack the place looks hastily built from rough-hewn boards and tin.

8. Many people assume that economic equality has become a fact of American workers' lives but the truth is that women and minorities are paid considerably less than white men who perform comparable jobs.
9. I've seen it happen many times, "city slickers" move in and criticize the pace of small-town life at first then begin to experience just how much more relaxing life is here.
10. Steamboat Springs, Colorado, is not only for the winter ski enthusiast it is also a great place for summer hikers and cyclists.

Exercise 21--Editing Irregular Verbs

Edit the following sentences for errors in irregular verb forms. If a sentence is correct, write "correct" after it. To learn the correct forms of irregular verbs, see 13a in *The Ready Reference Handbook*. Answers to lettered items appear in the back of this booklet. Example:

> **As we sat down to dinner, I was momentarily dazzled by all the forks and spoons ~~laying~~ *lying* next to each plate.**

a. Joel lamented that he had lost his most prized possession, the wristwatch his father had gave him just before he died.
b. On sale this week at the Edgewood Orchard Gallery are the most beautiful scarves, each one weaved from natural fibers.
c. When the police seen the thief's footprints leading away from the river, they knew at once where he had hid the money from the robbery.
d. The minister rose from his seat and lead the congregation in the first hymn of the service.
e. The committee has selected its final candidates, interviewed them, evaluated their strengths, and wrote out its recommendation.

1. I could have swore that when the clerk rung up our bill, he made an error on purpose.
2. The voters have once again spoke against higher taxes and sent this message: "If something's not broke, then don't try to fix it!"

3. The Environmental Policy Center claims that Americans have chosen urban sprawl over careful urban planning, and as a result we are losing some of our best farmland to housing tracts.
4. Michael Jordan was so confident of his basketball skills and so wealthy that he could afford to set out a season while he tried his hand at baseball.
5. When I came home from work yesterday, I discovered that someone had snuck through my back yard, broke a window on my garage, and stole my lawn mower.
6. Judy and Pat laid on the beach for two hours before remembering they had forgot to bring any sunscreen with them.
7. Has any woman ever ran a mile in four minutes or less?
8. When his car slid into the ditch and rolled over, Jerry was badly shook up but not injured.
9. I've just received a letter warning me that if I haven't payed for my reservations by June first, I'll loose the vacation opportunity of a lifetime.
10. After laying in bed for two weeks with the flue and bronchitis, Peter decided that his boredom was worse than his discomfort.

Exercise 22--Editing Verb Tenses

Edit the following sentences to correct errors in verb tense. If a sentence is correct, write "correct" after it. To learn to use verb tenses correctly , see 13b in *The Ready Reference Handbook.* Answers to lettered items appear in the back of this booklet. Example:

had chosen

Nick told his advisor that he ^ already ~~chose~~ ^ his major, geology.

a. We returned home from California by the same route that took us there.

b. More movies were made of *Romeo and Juliet* than of any other Shakespeare play.

c. At Matt and Joe's funeral, we laughed as much as we cried, remembering all the good times we had with them.

d. It wasn't until a year later that Mia discovered what had caused her friends to abandon her without a word.

e. Throughout the history of the United States, minorities and women were discriminated against.

1. When Stacy returned to Houston after ten years in Asia, she wanted to visit the house she once lived in.
2. By now, more than 200,000 have died of AIDS, more than three times the number of Americans who had died during the Vietnam War.
3. In Shakespeare's *Romeo and Juliet,* two adolescents who belonged to rival families fell in love and were secretly married in spite of their parents' opposition.
4. Cars were backed up for miles on the freeway, and thirty minutes had passed before John had reached the site of the accident.
5. Inside the nest were four tiny rabbits buried in fur that was shed by their mother.
6. It was the Polish astronomer and cleric Copernicus who discovered that the earth revolves around the sun.
7. Since our loud argument about politics, Jeffrey and I never spoke another word to each other.
8. March 24th dawned cloudy, cold, and rainy, just as the weather forecaster predicted.
9. Six years passed since my parents' divorce, and they were finally beginning to be civil to each other.
10. Julian Jaynes speculated in his controversial book *The Origins of Consciousness* that early humans developed spoken language at the same time they were evolving consciousness.
11. As Alicia grew, her grandparents tried to teach her what they were taught as children in Mexico and Italy.
12. The French chemist Lavoisier named both hydrogen and oxygen and showed how they combined to form water.

13. The police officer observed that the patio door had been opened from the inside and was probably used for the burglar's exit.

14. Our research group planned to finish our experiment by the end of last week.

15. After the game, Paul sat down wearily next to Kerry and asked how well he did.

Exercise 23--Editing Verb Forms

Edit the following sentences for omitted verbs and missing or incorrect verb endings. If a sentence is correct, write "correct" after it. To learn the correct use of *be, have,* and *do* and when to use the *-s, -es, -d,* and *-ed* verb endings, see 13c, d, and e in *The Ready Reference Handbook.* Answers to lettered items appear in the back of this booklet. Example:

The four gold medals Jesse Owens won at the 1936 olympics show that he
is
the greatest track and field athlete of all time.
^

a. My aunt and uncle have recently retire to a small town in Arkansas charmingly name Mountain Home.

b. Darren use to believe that people on welfare are all lazy bums.

c. We would of been here hours ago if the mechanic had fix the car the way he was suppose to.

d. Do he have the slightest idea how inconsiderate he is to be doing something else when people trying to talk to him?

e. A scientist claims to have produced a biological antipollution agent that literally eats solid waste materials.

1. The Regal Music Company have just release its CD collection of the greatest Chicago and Mississippi blues hits of the 1950s and 60s.

2. Yesterday on the radio a dietitian announce that by the year 2050 one hundred percent of Americans will be overweight.

3. As Sheri read her great-grandmother's diary, she try to imagine what it must of been like to live in the early 1900s.

4. You might not believe it, but we been brewing our own beer in our basement for the past three years.
5. Rural people are increasingly isolated because Amtrak has discontinue service to their communities.
6. I always thought that a voter was suppose to be a register Democrat or Republican to vote in a primary election.
7. Like almost everyone, Linda don't know how many homeless people are children.
8. He were trying to light the gas fireplace when it exploded with a loud roar.
9. My friend Valda say she going to become a US citizen as soon as she eligible.
10. Two years ago, when I was still living at home, I couldn't of cared less whether I had any money.
11. The evidence suggests that he might have passed out from an epileptic seizure, swerved across the median, and struck the oncoming car.
12. Is it possible to imagine a society of unprejudice people?
13. In Washington State, archaeologists have discovered that Europeans might of come to North America long before Columbus, even before the Vikings.
14. Jamal first ask to see a menu but then quickly said he wanted only an ice tea and powder sugar doughnut.
15. The members of my department say they been giving Christmas donations to the FamCare Agency for more than five years.

Exercise 24--Choosing the Subjunctive or Indicative Mood

In the following sentences, fill in the blank with the appropriate subjunctive or indicative verb form. To learn more about the use of the subjunctive mood, see 13f in *The Ready Reference Handbook*. Answers to lettered items appear in the back of this booklet. Example:

Staring out the window at the bleak December sky, Jill wished she

were **in Florida.**
(was/were)

a. Attendance at the final Swirling Ants concert __________ (was/were) limited only by the size of the . auditorium.

b. The agent for the Swirling Ants quartet required that the number of concerts __________ (is/be) limited to two.

c. If I __________ (was/were) you, I would ask that the store owner __________ (return/returns) your check.

d. We could leave for work on time if everyone in the car pool __________ (was/were) punctual.

e. Most gun owners insist that the US Constitution __________ (give/gives) them the right to bear arms.

1. The apartment building owners insist that every tenant __________ (give/gives) them one month's rent as a security deposit.

2. If Lindy had known Jeremy __________ (was/were) coming, he would have set another place for dinner.

3. We requested that the florist __________ (deliver/delivers) the flowers before the ceremony __________ (begin/begins).

4. I have noticed that a good quarter back __________ (survey/surveys) the whole field before throwing a pass.

5. We recommend that an investigator __________ (survey/surveys) the damage before the homeowner files a claim.

Exercise 25--Editing Subject-Verb Agreement

Edit the following sentences to correct the identified errors of subject-verb agreement. If a sentence is correct, write "correct" after it. To learn about subject-verb agreement, see Chapter 14 in *The Ready Reference Handbook*. Answers to lettered items appear in the back of this booklet. Example:

Separated subject and verb:

The accuracy of political polls and public opinion surveys ~~are~~ *is* often doubted by skeptical voters.

a. *Separated subject and verb:* The economic well-being of virtually all of Stratford's 35,000 residents depend upon the success of their annual summer theater festival.

b. *Subject following the verb:* In New York City alone there is an estimated 250,000 intravenous drug users at risk of contracting AIDS.

c. *Compound subjects, singular verb:* New housing developments and the construction of a new highway has forced the area's deer population to forage in people's back yards.

d. *Compound subjects linked by* or *or* nor: Neither Florida nor California have much appeal to warm weather vacationers seeking adventure as well as sunshine.

e. *Indefinite pronoun subject:* Every one of the hot air balloons were decorated in bright, almost surreal colors.

1. *Collective noun as the subject:* Before the last note of the symphony had died, the audience were moving rapidly toward the exits.
2. Number *as a subject:* These days, the average number of years students take to earn their degrees are increasing from four to five or six or more.
3. *Plural nouns singular in meaning:* Never one of the easiest subjects, statistics has always been especially challenging to me.
4. *Relative pronoun as a subject:* Bill Clinton was the only one of the twentieth century Democratic presidents who were elected to a second term.
5. *Separated subject and verb:* A steaming bowl of chili, together with a platter of nachos and a slice of garlic bread, make a satisfying mid-winter meal.

Exercise 26--Editing Subject-Verb Agreement

Edit the following sentences to correct errors of subject-verb agreement. If a sentence is correct, write "correct" after it. To learn about subject-verb agreement, see Chapter 14 in *The Ready Reference Handbook.* Answers to lettered items appear in the back of this booklet. Example:

People who support term limits believe that twelve years in office are enough for any senator.

a. People who have been laid off or downsized know why economics are referred to as "the dismal science."

b. John Knudsen's paintings and sculpture is varied in technique but always devoted to urban themes.

c. The silence of the brooding, majestic pines and firs create a somber mood in the park's visitors.

d. In the past several months, there has been several cases of Dengue fever reported in Texas.

e. Commerce Secretary Ron Brown, in addition to his staff and the plane's crew, were killed in the crash.

1. Either the supervisor or the assembly line workers has the authority to stop production whenever necessary.
2. In a test to determine the harshness of shampoo, one of the test rabbit's eyes are held open with metal clips.
3. Each of the boxcars on the siding were covered with graffiti.
4. Inside the display cabinet was all sorts of unusual camping gear.
5. The fastest-growing group of impoverished American children are those whose parents have jobs.
6. Nearly eighty percent of the American population need to reduce their calories and increase their exercise.
7. Keith is one of the few people I know who actually enjoys airports.
8. Neither of those descriptions do justice to the colors of this year's autumn.

9. Not one of the members of my division were in the office when the personnel chief came in with news of the layoffs.
10. It is increasingly difficult to persuade Americans that most government regulation and taxation is beneficial.
11. A number of unanticipated causes, such as the overgrazing of cattle, was responsible for the dust storms of the 1930s.
12. Loud squabbles between social classes, regional battles for government pork barrel projects, and legislators' quest for power betrays the founding principles of this nation.
13. The class were just taking their seats when a stranger walked in to announce that their professor was ill.
14. In the back of the barn, covered with dust, was a 1932 Model A Ford and a rare Indian motorcycle.
15. Furniture constructed of walnut, cherry, or maple have the most lustrous finish.

Exercise 27--Editing Pronoun-Antecedent Agreement

Edit the following sentences to correct errors of pronoun-antecedent agreement. If a sentence is correct, write "correct" after it. To learn about pronoun-antecedent agreement, see Chapter 15 in *The Ready Reference Handbook.* Answers to lettered items appear in the back of this booklet. Example:

> *personal trainers begin*
> **To determine optimal exercise heart rate, ~~a personal trainer begins~~ by**
> *their* *-s* ^
> **weighing ~~his~~ client and taking their pulse.**
> ^ ^

a. When my parents sat me down to tell me of their divorce, I heard their words, but none of it made any sense.

b. Everyone experiences depression at some point in their lives.

c. Hideaway Resort is widely known for their inexpensive but comfortable and activity-filled vacations.

d. Neither Eric nor the other swimmers could remember when they last saw Jean with them near the raft.

e. Unable to speak the language and knowing little about local customs, we did what anyone would do to protect themselves from con artists and thieves.

1. Our company encourages each employee to contribute one percent of their salary to a charitable organization.
2. In psychology class last year, I learned how memory works, how to retain what I have learned, and how to remember them when I need them.
3. In the Pacific Northwest, loggers and environmentalists have been arguing for years about whether to protect the northern spotted owl. They have become an endangered species because they depend for their habitat upon the old-growth timber so prized by logging companies.
4. I told everyone on the tour to relax when they met the king, to be themselves, and not to imitate the behavior of someone they're not.
5. In cases of passive euthanasia, a person has signed a living will indicating that if they are terminally ill or mortally injured, they should not be resuscitated.
6. The mob scattered and ran when it saw the police cars.
7. Studies in nursing homes reveal that the more education one has, the easier it is for them to adjust to advancing age.
8. As soon as teenagers turn sixteen, they are able to drive, and of course they want their own cars. At this time, parents seldom argue because they would rather have their child drive his own car than have to drive them wherever they want to go. Unfortunately, however, his first car is usually a hazard for him and everyone else on the road.
9. Recently, the government has begun to re-examine the regulations they originally created to protect citizens.

10. A student who stays in school, studies hard, and earns their diploma ought to receive a salary equal to the professional athlete who dropped out after his sophomore year.
11. Someone left me an unsigned e-mail message telling me that they couldn't come to this week's jam session.
12. For the first two days of the cruise, nobody became seasick, and so they ate and drank as much as they pleased.
13. No matter what their parents do to preserve their culture, an immigrant child is inevitably drawn to the culture of their peers and the habits of their new country.
14. Throughout the years, they have been an insurance company that not only offers a fine annuity program but continues to serve the client after their enrollment.
15. The part-time staff staged a large demonstration outside the president's office protesting its low pay and lack of benefits.

Exercise 28--Editing Pronoun Reference

Edit the following sentences to correct errors in pronoun reference. If a sentence is correct, write "correct" after it. To learn about the reference of pronouns, see Chapter 16 in *The Ready Reference Handbook.* Answers to lettered items appear in the back of this booklet. Example:

> **My parents wouldn't let me play ice hockey because they thought it was too**
> *Their refusal*
> **dangerous. ~~This~~ just made me want to play even more.**
> ∧

a. Karen had no desire to taste the goat's milk, and she was certain she didn't want to milk it.
b. Betty told Adele the exciting news about her winning lottery ticket.
c. Morale at my company is low because employees don't know one another or understand any job besides their own. This makes it difficult to increase productivity.
d. Avid readers should stop at the Book Nook; they have weekly specials on adult and children's books of all kinds.
e. In today's highly mobile society, you can easily lose touch with family members which have been forced to relocate as part of their jobs.

1. Eczema is characterized by reddened skin, itching, blisters, crusting, and scaling. This can be extreme and even lead to emotional disturbance.
2. The lives of experimental animals are taken for specific reasons, and it is done humanely, as quickly and painlessly as possible.
3. To help pay my tuition last year, I worked two jobs--which, of course, meant that I rarely had time to study.
4. During hay fever season Becky is miserable nearly every day, and it shows.
5. According to the teachings of the Catholic Church, if you display pride, lust, anger, or sloth, you have committed mortal sin.
6. At our college, they have transformed the humble library into the pompous-sounding "Learning Resources Center."
7. Many single mothers' most difficult choice is whether she will have an abortion, give it up for adoption, or try to raise it alone.
8. Last semester, for the first time in my college career, I earned all A's and B's and made the Dean's List. The primary reason for this was my night clerk's job at a local motel that gave me lots of study time.
9. On our first date, Carlos brought me a large bouquet of flowers, which no one had ever done for me.
10. Recently passed Bill 101 makes French the only officially recognized language in Quebec. This has had profound effects on businesses, schools, and other organizations.
11. For most businesses, larger markets mean a faster turnover of inventory, which means higher profits for them and lower prices for consumers.
12. Throughout his last year with the Springfield Bees basketball team, Clyde Griffiths was involved in a bitter contract dispute with them.
13. When people suffer from alienation, they feel isolated from society and resentful because of it.

14. In the town where I spent my first year in the Peace Corps, they had no telephones, so all news came through the tiny post office.

15. Two years after my parents' divorce, my father started a new family. I suppose I should be generous, but it bothered me.

Exercise 29--Editing Pronoun Case Forms

Edit the following sentences to correct errors in pronoun case. If a sentence is correct, write "correct" after it. To learn about pronoun case forms, see Chapter 17 in *The Ready Reference Handbook*. Answers to lettered items appear in the back of this booklet. Example:

him and me
The instructions given to ~~he and I~~ were not very clear.
^

a. It should be obvious that we students prefer a more generous scholarship program.

b. Janet, Jeffrey, Patricia, and myself will be pleased to help with the Oxfam Fund Drive.

c. As me and my two friends were setting up out tents at sunset, we looked up and saw four or five black bears near the edge of the woods.

d. You may not see the difference, but us conscientious objectors call ourselves "draft resisters" not "draft dodgers."

e. I was delighted when Edward gave my husband and I two tickets to the new Tom Stoppard play.

1. Lindsey deserves all the credit for us winning the championship.

2. Three days after the explosion, rescue workers began hearing faint sounds indicating that her and her two brothers were still alive under the debris.

3. People tend to overlook Jessie, but the one person most responsible for our department's success is she.

4. The assignment directs two volunteers, in this case Harry and I, to give a five-minute talk on the death of Edgar Allan Poe.

5. The park rangers discovered my brother and I walking cautiously along the narrow path above Look Away Falls.
6. For us to spend another dime subsidizing wealthy farmers is foolish; they can help theirselves.
7. Marie has more allergies than me, and that explains why she doesn't enjoy country walks as much as me.
8. Disaster was averted solely because of the alertness of we engineers on the night shift.
9. I'm sorry to say that between my step-father and I there are seldom many pleasant words.
10. The counsellor helped my husband and I resolve the problems threatening our marriage.

Exercise 30--Choosing **Who** *or* **Whom, Whoever** *or* **Whomever**

Fill in the blanks with *who* or *whom, whoever* or *whomever*. To learn about these pronouns, see 17e in *The Ready Reference Handbook.* Answers to lettered items appear in the back of this booklet. Example:

Whom (who/whom) did the Vice President ask to be her new assistant?

a. Three of the people __________ (who/whom) the grand jury has identified have long criminal records.

b. In politics today, it's not necessarily the person __________ (who/whom) shakes the most hands __________ (who/whom) wins the election.

c. During the holidays, we give clothing and food to ______________ (whoever/whomever) needs them the most.

d. __________ (who/whom) was nominated for this years best actor award?

e. The people __________ (who/whom) receive the best medical care are usually the ones __________ (who/whom) can afford to pay for it.

1. Among the celebrities __________ (who/whom) we hope will attend the gallery's opening are Earl and Leslie Diamond.

2. We Americans tend to admire _______________ (whoever/whomever) makes the most money, not necessarily _______________ (whoever/whomever) does the most good.

3. Professor Wilson, __________ (who/whom) many expect to retire in the near future, says he will teach for at least five more years.

4. Was it he __________ (who/whom) you saw fleeing the scene of the crime?

5. In a cynic's democracy, it's up to the politicians and the powerful to decide __________ (who/whom) we will elect to lead us.

Exercise 31--Editing Adjectives and Adverbs

Edit the following sentences for the correct use of adjectives and adverbs. If a sentence is correct, write "correct" after it. To learn to use adjectives and adverbs correctly, see Chapter 18 in *The Ready Reference Handbook*. Answers to lettered items appear in the back of this booklet. Example:

> **In this era of corporate downsizing, trust is not something that comes**
> *automatically*
> **~~automatic~~ to workers and management.**
> ^

a. Judy's chocolate chip holiday cookies smell wonderful and taste delicious.

b. The man in the clown suit and greasy makeup looked at me peculiar.

c. The man in the clown suit and greasy makeup looked peculiar.

d. Joshua had the most happiest of childhoods.

e. On the balance beam, Sharon performed good.

1. To burn fat quick, overweight weekend athletes should exercise slow and consistent.
2. When the magician Houdini was a child, he and his father worked steady but unprofitably as tailors in a New York sweatshop.
3. Together the father and son earned barely enough to keep their family alive.
4. Once you understand the strategies of a sport, the physical skills come much more easier.

5. Artists of ancient Rome depicted life after death as based on earthly life. Similar, artists of the Renaissance painted their images of heaven and hell based on the life they saw around them.
6. When Ann and Janet went to London, where drivers drive on the left side of the road, they learned real quick to look both ways before stepping off a curb.
7. Unless I make an outline before I begin writing, I hardly never produce smooth flowing sentences.
8. In the early morning sun, the little village in the valley looked like the most perfect place on earth.
9. I know I treated him bad, but I felt pretty badly myself when he insulted her in front of her friends.
10. Alice Munro writes short stories about popular, everyday subjects, but she looks really deep into those subjects.
11. Cheryl's carelessness has had a tremendous harmful impact on people around her.
12. Whenever I was having trouble learning a new skating routine, my grandmother would remind me that nothing good ever comes easy.
13. Bonnie was denied health insurance because she had been diagnosed has having previous existing health problems.
14. The melting snow has caused flood waters to rise nearly equal on both sides of the levee.
15. At Eagle Mountain Ski Resort, a t-bar and two pony lifts are available to carry skiers to the top of the slopes as quick as possible.

Exercise 32--Editing Faulty Parallelism

Edit the following sentences to correct faulty parallelism. If a sentence is correct, write "correct" after it. To learn about parallel form, see Chapter 19 in *The Ready Reference Handbook*. Answers to lettered items appear in the back of this booklet. Example:

The marks of a good restaurant are a choice of dishes seldom prepared at home and ~~where~~ *that* ingredients are fresh and flavorful.

a. The campsites in many national parks have electric and running water.

b. According to a recent Canadian study, the keys to financial success are education, to work hard, and not take risks.

c. Today, many college students use telephones to register for their classes and reserve seats for special on-campus events.

d. As my father's cancer worsened, he debated whether to end the painful chemotherapy or continuing to battle his terrible disease.

e. Erin would rather spend her weekend surfing the Internet on her computer than dance the night away at a fancy club.

1. I recommend renting *Night of the Living Dead* for its simple plot, its suspensefulness, and it has vivid horror scenes.
2. After lengthy negotiations, the employees and management agreed that there would be no layoffs and wages would be increased by four percent a year.
3. Richard Rodriguez is an insightful writer who not only understands the frustrations of learning a second language, but he also vividly portrays the immigrant experience in America.
4. To begin rehabbing my house, I had to learn how to hang sheet rock, paneling, know which screws and nails to use for each job, paint, patch holes, plumbing and minor electrical repairs.
5. Although my house needed numerous repairs, it had a new roof, aluminum siding, all new storm windows, new electrical service, a new septic tank had recently been put in, and it had a beautiful yard.

6. The most typical immigrant I interviewed was a young man, twenty-four years old and single, sends money home to his family, and wants to remain in the U.S.
7. When Carol reached the panicky swimmer, she told him calmly that everything would be okay and to relax.
8. Whenever I have turned to my roommate for help, he has been negative, rude, uncooperative, and a troublemaker.
9. The doctors invited me into a small conference room, told me to sit down, and they had something serious to discuss with me.
10. In most writing, a good introduction makes the subject inviting but not revealing too much about it.

Exercise 33--Using the Active and Passive Voice

Rewrite each of the following sentences to change its voice as indicated in brackets. To learn to about active and passive voice verb forms, see 20a in *The Ready Reference Handbook.* Answers to lettered items appear in the back of this booklet. Example:

Bacteria cause leprosy. [Use the passive voice.]
Leprosy is caused by bacteria.

a. The cooling of molten lava produces igneous rocks. [Use the passive voice.]

b. The French impressionist Claude Monet painted enormous pictures of water lilies. [Use the passive voice.]

c. Ben will cook dinner for us. [Use the passive voice.]

d. Karate lessons are being taken by Roberta. [Use the active voice.]

e. Cosmic rays may be released into space by gigantic stellar explosions. [Use the active voice.]

1. Charles Dickens' novel *Great Expectations* should be read by every young adult. [Use the active voice.]

2. The Dead Sea Scrolls contain most of the biblical Old Testament and other Hebrew religious documents. [Use the passive voice.]

3. Jean will have written more than 100,000 words when she finishes her first novel. [Use the passive voice.]

4. Ever since our department's reorganization, my supervisor has been demanding increased productivity. [Use the passive voice.]

5. Weekly meetings are held by the office supervisor so that questions from her staff can be answered by her. [Use the active voice.]

Exercise 34--Editing the Active and Passive Voice

Edit the following sentences for ineffective uses of the active and passive voice. If a sentence uses the active or passive voice effectively, write "correct" after it. Be prepared to explain your decisions. To learn about the active and passive voice, see 20a in *The Ready Reference Handbook*. Answers to lettered items appear in the back of this booklet. Example:

> Beth spent
>
> **In the weeks before her vacation, weeks ~~were spent by Beth~~ in the library reading books about the Greek Islands.**

a. Between 1900 and 1972, U.S. courts condemned more than 150 innocent men to die, and executioners executed at least 23 of them.

b. A polyester gene has been inserted into a cotton plant by genetic engineers in order to grow wrinkle-free fibers as warm as wool.

c. Care should be taken by writers of arguments to use only facts and generally accepted truths.

d. An iceberg the size of Rhode Island has recently broken away from the coast of Antarctica and may drift northward for ten years before melting.

e. The massive iceberg is estimated to tower 100 to 160 feet above the water and 1,000 feet below.

1. In the South, many poor blacks were once prevented from voting by the poll tax, a tax on the act of voting.
2. Even before she spoke, I could tell by the look in her eyes that her audition had been successful.
3. When my brother's large and hungry family comes to our house for Thanksgiving, "May we have seconds?" are the words heard most frequently around our dinner table.
4. All the information for my report had finally been compiled and arranged in a logical order.
5. Plans for the merger are being carefully reviewed by the presidents of both companies so that it will proceed smoothly.

Exercise 35--Emphasizing with Subordination

Combine or rewrite the following sentences, using subordination to emphasize major ideas and de-emphasize minor ideas. Follow bracketed instructions when they appear. For some items more than one correct revision is possible. To learn about subordination, see 20b in *The Ready Reference Handbook*. Answers to lettered items appear in the back of this booklet. Example:

> *Since* *when*
>
> **~~In~~ 1977, the United States resumed the practice of capital punishment, ~~and~~ ~~since that date~~ sixty-one condemned men have been discovered to be innocent and released from death row.**

a. The greatest decline in cancer death rates has been among African-American men, yet their death rates are still higher than those of whites. [Subordinate with a subordinating conjunction.]

b. Stress and depression trigger the release of hormones. These hormones may cause brittle bones, infections, and even cancer. [Subordinate with a relative pronoun.]

c. On January 30, 1969, the Beatles gave their final live performance, and it was an impromptu set on the roof of their London Apple Corps offices. [Subordinate with an appositive.]

d. More than two dozen glaciers flow down the slopes of Mount Rainier, and they end at the timberline at an elevation of 6,500 feet. [Subordinate with a participial phrase.]

e. The great Apache war leader Geronimo was actually named Goyathlay, and this name means "one who yawns" in Apache. [Subordinate with a participial phrase.]

1. Agricultural plants may be genetically altered through a transfer process. The process is called particle bombardment. [Subordinate with a participial phrase.]

2. Mexico City is the world's largest city, and it is one of the most polluted. [Subordinate with an appositive.]

3. The Mexico City subway system has alleviated some of the city's traffic congestion, but 3.5 million cars, trucks, buses, and motorcycles still belch poisonous fumes into the air. [Subordinate with a subordinating conjunction.]

4. Tom Thumb's real name was Charles Sherwood Stratton. He was born in 1838 and, as an adult, grew to be only forty inches tall. [Subordinate with a relative pronoun.]

5. In the third century BC, Shi Huangdi built the Great Wall of China. The wall linked earlier walls. These walls had been constructed to mark Chinese territory and repel invaders. [Subordinate with a participial phrase.]

6. In the future, cancer death rates will probably increase. More people will live to advanced ages. During this period of life, cancer is a common occurrence.

7. The elephant is the world's largest living land animal. It can reach 10 feet in height and weigh up to 3,500 pounds.

8. Recently, 200 African elephants were found slaughtered in the Congo, and they were the victims of ivory poachers.

9. Poachers threaten the extinction of African elephants. They have slaughtered more than half of all African elephants in the last ten years.

10. *The Canterbury Tales* was written by Geoffrey Chaucer in the late 14th century, and it is collection of twenty-four tales. Pilgrims supposedly told these tales to pass the time during a pilgrimage. They were going to the shrine of St. Thomas à Beckett in Canterbury.

Exercise 36--Emphasizing with Coordination

Combine the following sentences, using coordination to emphasize related ideas. For some items more than one correct revision is possible. To learn about coordination, see 20c in *The Ready Reference Handbook*. Answers to lettered items appear in the back of this booklet. Example:

> refers ... but
>
> **Brownian motion ~~does~~ not ~~refer~~ to a new dance step~~. It refers~~ to the erratic, zigzag motion of microscopic particles.**

a. Barry and Sheri telephoned to say that they were unable to attend this year's community clean-up day. Two hours later they arrived with rakes, brooms, and garbage bags.

b. Improved urban highways are reducing commuter travel times. They are also reducing accident rates.

c. The evidence indicates that capital punishment does not prevent murders. It is disproportionally applied to the poor and minorities. It should be abolished.

d. Strong head winds did not prevent Jerry Mount and his crew from completing their first race to Mackinaw Island. A badly ripped mainsail didn't prevent them, either.

e. The Mason-Dixon line is popularly considered the dividing line between the northern and southern states. Actually, it marks the border between Pennsylvania on the north and Maryland and West Virginia on the south.

1. Quasars are the brightest objects in the universe. The brightest is 30,000 times brighter than the Milky Way.
2. They emit their energy as radio waves. They emit it as visible light. And they also emit it as gamma rays and X-rays.
3. Smoking sharpens short-term learning. It also sharpens short-term memory. Smoking also greatly increases the risk of heart disease. It also increases the risk of cancer.
4. There are approximately 8,000 museums in the US. They are devoted to every aspect of American culture. There are museums devoted to roller skating. There are museums devoted to dentistry. There is a museum devoted to the fur trade. There is museum devoted to the alphabet. There is a museum devoted to the Mountain Man. There is a museum devoted to rattlesnakes. There is even a museum devoted to barbed wire.
5. The Ganges River flows across northern India. Then it runs through Bangladesh until, after 1,600 miles, it reaches the Bay of Bengal.
6. Carrie Amelia Moore Nation was known for fiery anti-drinking sermons. She was known for destroying saloons with her hatchet.
7. She preached frequently in prisons. She concluded from her observations that liquor and crime were related.
8. Her audiences ignored her sermons against drinking. She turned to direct action.

9. Armed with her hatchet, she entered Kansas saloons. She smashed bottles. She smashed furnishings.

10. She took her message to England to publicize her cause. She returned to the U.S. two years later. She was ill. She was unable to continue her mission.

Exercise 37--Emphasizing with Subordination and Coordination

Using subordination and subordination, combine or rewrite the following sentences. When appropriate, use both in one item. For some items more than one correct revision is possible. To learn about subordination, see 20b and c in *The Ready Reference Handbook.* Answers to lettered items appear in the back of this booklet. Example:

> **Brownian motion was first observed in 1827 by the English botanist Robert Brown~~. He~~ , who was observing the contents of pollen grains.**

a. Lightning is usually associated with thunderstorms. It may also be produced by snowstorms, sandstorms, even the clouds over erupting volcanoes.

b. Ball lightning is a spherical flash. The flash varies in size from three to three hundred feet in diameter. It lasts less than five seconds.

c. The abominable snowman is a giant creature. It is also known as the "yeti." It supposedly roams the mountains at night. He is looking for victims.

d. It is described as having an upright posture. It has a covering of black to reddish hair. And it has the appearance of a bear, ape, or human.

e. In one version of the story of Lady Godiva, she was observed by only one person. This was a tailor. He was the original Peeping Tom. He was struck blind by what he saw.

1. Alvin Straight couldn't see well enough to get a driver's license. He rode his lawn tractor across Iowa and part of Wisconsin. He wanted to visit his sick brother.

2. He didn't want to fly. He didn't want to take a bus to his brother's home. His only option was his lawn tractor.

3. In July 1994, Mr. Straight set out. He pulled a trailer loaded with gear, gas, and food.

4. In the year 610, the prophet Muhammad was in a cave on a mountain near Mecca. He had a dream. The dream called upon him to preach a message. The message was given to him by God.

5. Hiram Rhoades is a figure unknown to most Americans. But he was the first African-American to serve in the U.S. Senate. He filled the seat once held by Jefferson Davis. He was the President of the Confederacy.

Exercise 38--Emphasizing with Repetition

For each of the following, write a sentence that uses the identified word, word ending, phrase, or clause in a series of emphatic repetitions. To learn about emphatic repetition, see 20d in *The Ready Reference Handbook.* The list of topics on p. 138 will give you ideas for your writing.

1. A repeated noun, verb, adjective, or adverb. Example:

    When I was a child, I spoke as a child, I understood as a child, thought as a child, but when I became a man, I put away childish things.

    --St. Paul

2. *No, not,* or *never*

3. A series of phrases each beginning with a preposition (*in, on, of, by, over,* and so forth). For a complete list, see 8f in *The Ready Reference Handbook.*

4. A series of phrases each beginning with a participle (a verb-like word ending in *-ing, -ed, -en, -n,* or *-t*). For more on participles, see 8c and 10a2 in *The Ready Reference Handbook.*

5. *To*

Exercise 39--Emphasizing with Periodic Sentences

Complete each of the following sentence openers as a periodic sentence, ending with its main clause or main idea. To learn about periodic sentences, see 20e2 in *The Ready Reference Handbook.* Example:

> **If a man can write a better book, preach a better sermon, or make a better mousetrap than his neighbor, though he build his house in the woods, the world will make a beaten path to his door.**
>
> --Ralph Waldo Emerson

1. Begin with *Early in the morning . . .* or *Late in the evening . . . .*

2. Begin with a participle (a verb-like word ending in *-ing, -ed, -en, -n,* or *-t*). For more on participles, see 8c8 and 10a2 in *The Ready Reference Handbook.*

3. Begin with a subordinating conjunction (*after, although, because, if, since, when,* and so forth). For a list of subordinating conjunctions, see 8g3 in *The Ready Reference Handbook.*

4. Begin with a list or series.

5. Begin with a phrase headed by a preposition (*in, on, of, by, over,* and so forth). For a complete list, see 8f in *The Ready Reference Handbook.*

Exercise 40--Variety: Combining Choppy Sentences

Edit the following paragraphs to vary sentence length and structure. Combine short, choppy sentences using subordination and coordination. To learn how to vary sentences, see 21a and b in *The Ready Reference Handbook.* More than one effective revision is possible.

a. Most of us can heavily influence our chances of becoming cancer victims. This was the conclusion of a recent study by the Harvard University School of Public Health. This study considered the causes of cancer deaths. It identified unhealthy choices as the cause of most of these deaths. Smoking causes thirty percent. Poor diet and obesity cause thirty percent. Lack of exercise causes five percent. Environmental carcinogens cause only a small percentage of cancer deaths. Family history causes a small percentage. Virus causes a small percentage. Alcohol causes a small percentage. And so does socioeconomic status cause only a small percentage.

1. The study recommends a few simple changes in our habits and lifestyles. These will considerably lower cancer risks. The most obvious recommendation concerns smoking.

Smokers should quit their habit. Other recommendations concern changes in our diet. One recommendation is to include more fruits and vegetables in our diet. These will reduce the risk of cancer of the lungs, esophagus, and larynx. More beans and grains should be consumed. These products will reduce cancer of the stomach and pancreas. Less red meat and animal fats should be eaten. These are linked to colorectal, prostate, and breast cancers. More exercise will reduce the risk of these cancers. And we should avoid the sun's ultraviolet rays whenever possible. These are responsible for 90 percent of skin cancers.

Exercise 41--Variety: Dividing Rambling Sentences

Divide the following loose, rambling sentences, using subordination and coordination to emphasize important ideas. More than one effective revision is possible. To learn how to divide sentences, see 21c in *The Ready Reference Handbook.* Answers to lettered items appear in the back of this booklet.

a. From the early 19th century to the 1860s, the Oregon Trail was the primary route to the American west, carrying thousands of pioneers nearly 2,000 miles from Independence Missouri to the rich farmland of the Willamette Valley in Oregon country and ending at Fort Vancouver, the site of modern Vancouver, Washington.

b. The main route ran west from Independence and then northwest to Fort Kearney, then west again along the Platte and North Platte rivers to Fort Laramie, crossing the Rockies by South Pass and veering north to Fort Hall, where it picked up the Snake River flowing to Fort Boise, in what is now Idaho, and then finally swung northwest to the Columbia River, which the pioneers usually navigated by raft to Fort Vancouver.

1. Explorers, fur trappers, and traders were the first travelers of the trail early in the 19th century, followed by Marcus Whitman and a group of missionary families, who opened up new routes in 1836 and were so impressed by what they found in Oregon that they reported

their discoveries to the East and encouraged others to come and establish farms in the rich valley.

2. The reaction to their reports was the "Oregon Fever" that broke out in the spring of 1843, as nearly 1,000 men, women, and children gathered in Independence with their wagons to begin the six-month journey west, and continued until, by 1846, more than 6,000 people had traveled the trail, but the discovery of gold in California in 1848 quickly reduced the number of travelers, and by the 1860s the original flood had diminished to a trickle.
3. To make their trek, the pioneers organized themselves into small companies and agreed to accept the strict discipline necessary to meet the perils of the route, hostile Indians, cholera epidemics, grass fires, storms, floods, and also the boredom of vast stretches of empty country and the fatigue and hunger resulting from diminished supplies of nourishing food.

Exercise 42--Varying Sentence Structure

Use the instructions in each of the following items to practice varied sentence structure. To learn to vary the structure of sentences, see 21e in *The Ready Reference Handbook.*

1. Open a sentence with an adverb. To learn about adverbs, see 8e in *The Ready Reference Handbook.*
2. Open a sentence with a participial phrase that modifies a nearby word. To learn about participial phrases, see 10a2 in *The Ready Reference Handbook.*
3. Open with a prepositional phrase. To learn about prepositional phrases, see 10a1 in *The Ready Reference Handbook.*
4. Open with an introductory series followed by a dash connecting the series to the main clause of the sentence.
5. Open with an appositive. To learn about appositives, see 10a3 in *The Ready Reference Handbook.*
6. Open with an absolute. To learn about absolutes, see 10a4 in *The Ready Reference Handbook.*
7. Invert the order of a sentence, putting the verb and related words before the subject.

Exercise 43--Editing for Varied Sentence Structure

Edit the following sentences to vary the common subject + verb pattern. More than one effective revision is possible. To learn to vary the structure of sentences, see 21e in *The Ready Reference Handbook*. Answers to lettered items appear in the back of this booklet. Example:

> *Gradually, the*
> **~~The~~ gap between the wealthy and poor widened ~~gradually,~~ until by 1992 the annual income of the wealthiest one percent of Americans was greater than that of the bottom forty percent.**

a. More than five million Americans work for the prescribed minimum wage, often performing the most menial tasks.

b. The original purpose of the minimum wage was to assure the basic health and well being of workers.

c. Many low-wage workers are forced to turn to relatives' charity and government assistance when they reach the end of the month and bills pile up.

d. Part-time workers will outnumber full-time workers within the next ten years.

e. Manpower Incorporated, an employment agency providing temporary workers, is now the nation's major private employer.

1. Nearly all fast foods are deep-fat fried, from the potatoes to the chicken to the apple pie.
2. French fries contain less sodium, surprisingly, than almost everything else on the fast food menu.
3. Fast food contains a number of unappetizing ingredients, including ground-up chicken skin, yellow dye number five, fish paste, and beef tallow.
4. Double and triple cheeseburgers are the monsters of the fast-food horror story, containing up to a quarter cup of fat.
5. Consumers should insist that fast food companies switch from animal fat to vegetable oil as a favor to their arteries.

Exercise 44--Editing Faulty Predication and Mixed Constructions

Edit the following sentences for illogically related subjects and predicates (faulty predication) and for mixed constructions (sentences written two ways at once). More than one correct revision is possible. To learn about faulty predication and mixed constructions, see 22a and b in *The Ready Reference Handbook.* Answers to lettered items appear in the back of this booklet. Example:

> *A gun license* *card*
> **~~Gun licensing~~ or registration should be viewed as a prized possession, not as an insult or document of suspicion.**

a. By removing the hood it makes it possible to lift the engine from the car.

b. Although Darrell Kaminsky is just beginning his professional basketball career, a prediction about his future shows the potential of soon becoming an All-Pro.

c. A number of waste disposal sites have begun to leak and will eventually have to be cleaned up and redumped.

d. Despite what some social critics say, America still exists as kind of melting pot in which we are all thrown into the pot to blend into one nation.

e. Back in the 1960s, when my parents were young, the economy seemed very plentiful.

1. If by telling the truth and saying what needs to be said is a crime, then I am guilty.
2. For many students, campus social clubs and academic organizations help to nurture a smooth transition through adolescence to adulthood.
3. The Yankees won the World Series this year because the pitching came through with a near-perfect performance and the coaching was patient and intelligent.
4. Blanche DuBois, although not physically as strong as her mortal enemy Stanley Kowalski, her will is firm.
5. My experience as a sales clerk was a failure because I couldn't persuade people to buy things I disliked.

6. A common form of professional irresponsibility is when an employee will lie to a superior to hide his or her laziness.
7. The consequences of wearing a seat belt are life-saving.
8. Although a car can strike an animal the size of a skunk or raccoon and not feel anything, an animal as large as a deer or moose can destroy it.
9. Unfortunately, the first members of the audience to arrive the ushers directed them to the worst seats in the house.
10. When I waited tables in a coffee house, the serious talkers were usually too busy talking that they seldom even heard me ask to take their orders.

Exercise 45--Editing Faulty Comparisons and Omitted Words

Edit the following sentences for illogical or incomplete comparisons and for omitted key words and function words. More than one correct revision is possible. To learn about comparisons and about necessary key words and function words, see 22c and d in *The Ready Reference Handbook.* Answers to lettered items appear in the back of this booklet. Example:

> **When Joseph Sobek decided to pep up the game of paddle ball back in the 1940s,he redesigned the paddle, giving it strings and a handle shorter than**
> racket's
> **a tennis ~~racket.~~**
> ∧

a. After hours of trudging through thick brush and damp, soggy ground, Eric and Emily finally came upon a small clearing where they could set up their tent.
b. Some people assume that because no one in their family has had cancer, they won't either.
c. What I've discovered in my interviews is that children under the age of ten tend to have similar musical tastes as their parents.
d. There is no better time to observe mob behavior than professional sporting events.
e. The features of one computer are pretty much the same as every computer in the same price range.

1. In comparison with country judges and their strict attitude toward traffic offenses make urban court systems seem like a social welfare agency.
2. Don't be misled by the greater durability and reliability of American products. Their prices are lower, too.
3. The lesson to be learned is as long as people have strong character and a good lawyer, they shouldn't worry about surrendering to temptation.
4. What William Rathje argues, which I agree completely, is that the United States is currently recycling more waste than necessary.
5. After our small plane leveled out at 5,000 feet, our flight became as smooth as any commercial airliner.
6. Salah affirmed that, as an orthodox Muslim, he believed and devoted to the wisdom of the Koran.
7. The Chicago Symphony has the greatest reputation than any other American orchestra.
8. Many have argued urinalysis undertaken without reasonable suspicion of drug use violates the constitutional limitation on search and seizure.
9. As an American of mixed heritage, I've found that prejudice is common, not only skin color but even geographical background.
10. When I want to feel depressed, I compare the lifestyles of the Kennedys, the Rockefellers, and the Astors to myself.

Exercise 46--Editing Mixed and Incomplete Messages

Edit the following sentences to correct problems of mixed and incomplete messages: faulty predication, mixed constructions, illogical or incomplete comparisons, and omitted key words and function words. More than one correct revision is possible. To learn about mixed and incomplete messages, see Chapter 22 in *The Ready Reference Handbook.* Answers to lettered items appear in the back of this booklet. Example:

> **Jeannetta said she preferred Professor Stone for her philosophy class**
> *than other philosopher instructors*
> **because he seems so much deeper and more knowledgeable.**
> ^

a. The Oklahoma City bombing was one of those tragic incidents where a nation's citizens are drawn together.

b. At the beginning of the test, the animal is placed in a small device where only its head protrudes from it.

c. Next, the animal's lower eyelids are pulled away from the eyes to form a cup in which shampoo is poured into the eyes.

d. She could only hope the jury would believe her account of the crime more than the prosecuting attorney.

e. No one I know admires the courage of the astronauts like me.

1. I know if you will just try Middle Eastern food, you will really enjoy it.
2. Ron, a close friend of mine since high school, has recently been diagnosed with an illness similar to my father.
3. It is because of Jim's passivity and indifference that has caused Lynda to look for another partner.
4. A good rule for sales personnel to remember is never to assume when talking with customers, do not take it for granted that they understand the product.
5. Active euthanasia is the form of mercy killing that most people do not agree with.
6. I observed my fellow passengers, their attention wandering toward the slowly turning ceiling fans, frowning at crying infants, or nodding off into an uneasy nap.
7. The latest government report on cigarettes concludes that women have a more difficult time quitting smoking than men.
8. By recognizing the near-certainty of his death from cancer has enabled my father to talk freely with his family for the first time in his life.

9. Even the most independent people feel loneliness at some point in their lives, whether it be a lost pet, a place they once lived, or someone they loved.
10. After repeated tests, researchers at the Bielaw Corporation have shown the picture is a cunning forgery.
11. As we set up camp, my husband conducted an organized procedure.
12. The primary reason for changing your own oil is the money you save vs. the quick lube businesses.
13. It was not until he nearly died in a severe automobile accident did Kerry recognize how careless and foolhardy he was.
14. Vincent van Gogh's painting style differs markedly from other postimpressionist painters.
15. Our block club is funded and affiliated with the Better Neighborhoods Organization.

Exercise 47--Editing Misplaced Modifiers

Edit the following sentences to correct misplaced modifiers. More than one correct revision is possible. To learn to place modifiers correctly, see 23a in *The Ready Reference Handbook.* Answers to lettered items appear in the back of this booklet. Example:

> *At the mouth of the cave, my*
> **~~My~~ brother constructed a little fire pit with rocks ~~at the mouth of the cave.~~**
> ∧

a. Albert only intended to just eat one chocolate-covered doughnut.

b. Dust began to thicken as the months passed on bookcases, file cabinets, and desks.

c. None of us thought night would ever come after paddling our canoes for twelve hours.

d. On the walls of the restaurant are large frames containing records and tapes plated with silver, gold, and platinum of famous musical artists.

e. I was walking back to the courthouse after a lunch break where I was serving on jury duty.

1. At the beginning of Hemingway's short story, two men walk into the diner named Al and Max, sit down, and gruffly order their food.

2. Finally, like Pavlov's salivating dogs, the dinner bell rang and hungry diners crowded the dining room doorway.
3. For the last three winters we have hardly had any snow.
4. Breckenridge, Colorado, is located nine miles south on Route 9 from Interstate 70 west of Denver.
5. Dr. Jesperson has suggested that to thoroughly understand Shakespeare's character Shylock, readers have to also understand anti-Semitism in Europe.
6. Many well-educated African-Americans have been forced to take jobs they are overqualified for just because of the color of their skin.
7. After five drinks apiece of scotch on the rocks, I was afraid my customers might try to drive themselves home.
8. For three days after my sister's surgery, an electronic monitoring device was taped to her chest which churned out all sorts of data.
9. Joe Christmas throughout the novel is trying to discover his identity.
10. I told Steven that I still had strong feelings for a fellow I had just broken up with as a hint that I didn't want to date him.

Exercise 48--Editing Dangling Modifiers

Edit the following sentences to correct dangling modifiers. More than one correct revision is possible. To learn how to avoid dangling modifiers, see 23b in *The Ready Reference Handbook*. Answers to lettered items appear in the back of this booklet. Example:

As I stepped
~~Stepping~~ into the foyer, a small Tiffany lamp greeted me with its luxurious
^
glow.

a. Chef Edgar has served dinners throughout Europe, including royalty.
b. From watching people toss it around in the park, playing with a frisbee must be very relaxing.
c. Hopefully, when the championship game is over, the victory flag will be hoisted over our stadium.

d. After reaching what lawyers call the age of accountability, life becomes more difficult for most young people.

e. Some jobs are not satisfying or glamorous but do pay good wages, a supermarket, for instance.

1. The sweat on our bodies beaded like water on a new wax job while walking back to the gym after a tough practice.
2. As a member of the Baby Boomer generation, Wilfred Owen's war poetry reminds me of those who were maimed in the Vietnam War.
3. Considerable controversy now surrounds the home medical test industry, which was introduced just a few months ago.
4. After reading the story three times, the same questions occurred to me again and again.
5. With mountain grades often over seven percent, even a light snowfall in the Rockies can cause dangerous road conditions.
6. When my family moved to New Hampshire last year, my history teacher gave me a friend's name who lived in Exeter.
7. In Streamwood recently, a sixteen-year-old girl's life was brutally taken from her after being abducted only fifty yards from her home.
8. Older people who have lived alone for many years frequently feel deep insecurity when entering a new relationship, whether a friend or lover.
9. After working at Inter-Tech for nearly thirty years, Sanford's dismissal was devastating.
10. During World War II, millions of young soldiers were killed, producing a severe shortage of men of marriageable age.

Exercise 49--Editing Faulty Shifts

Edit the following sentences to correct faulty shifts in point of view, number, tense, mood, tone, and discourse. More than one correct revision is possible. To learn to avoid faulty shifts, see Chapter 24 in *The Ready Reference Handbook.* Answers to lettered items appear in the back of this booklet. Example:

> **Students who want nothing to do with numbers usually change their ~~mind~~** *minds* **when they take Professor Held's college algebra course.**

a. One reason I enjoy rock 'n' roll so much is the joyful release the music offers you.

b. When I wasn't horseback riding or water skiing, many other recreational activities were provided by the resort staff for me to choose from.

c. Lenore believes that illegal immigrants should be deported and give their jobs to American citizens now receiving welfare payments.

d. Within the last five years, two of Decatur's largest manufacturing plants have shut down, and three others are heavily reducing their staff.

e. When a stager first begins to mix chemicals into paint, you must be careful to mix the correct chemicals in the proper amount.

1. All of my months of practice have finally paid off. As the audience applauds, chills of giddy delight run down your spine, and the feeling of triumph overwhelms you.
2. Senator Simon reminded his staff that when speaking to the press they should stick to the facts and care should be taken not to attack his opponent.
3. When most people draw up a living will, they usually indicate that if they are in a coma or terminally ill, do not resuscitate them.
4. I consider most automobile service managers to be a mechanic too old to crawl beneath a car.
5. At work Jerrod was the kindest, most helpful person imaginable, but then he goes home and abuses his wife and children.

6. Professor Nordstrom's physics course is certainly difficult, but his lectures could be understood if I paid more careful attention.
7. Husbands and wives should switch roles from time to time to add variety to their life.
8. Whenever my family goes to visit our uncle Buddy and his family, we feel as if we'd like to stay forever. Their casual, friendly manner makes you want to sit down, make yourself comfortable, and relax.
9. When falsely accused, most people will do whatever they can to prove they were innocent.
10. Betty was the exact opposite of her husband, who delighted in making people's life unpleasant.

Choosing Words

Exercise 50--Editing for Exact Words

Edit the following sentences to supply exact words and to correct problems of usage. More than one effective revision is possible. To learn how to choose exact words, see 25a, 25e, and 29 in *The Ready Reference Handbook.* Answers to lettered items appear in the back of this booklet. Example:

tenet
A basic ~~tenant~~ of mine is never to lend anything I might need someday.
^

a. By the end of the third day of the Battle of Gettysburg, the Confederate troops had been ultimately defeated.

b. Sunlight infiltrated the room through shear curtains on the patio doors.

c. Alot of people refuse to except scientific theories based on computer models rather than facts.

d. Of coarse, capitol punishment is intended to defer potentially deviate behavior.

e. Susan joined the local country club searching for perspective clients to buy her insurance policies.

1. Because the penalties for crime are so little, many criminals flaunt the law without fear of punishment.
2. Kevin is disinterested in hearing anyone's opinion but his own.
3. The judge instructed the jury implicitly to disregard the proceeding testimony.
4. After chatting for awhile, the two men shook hands and left the restaurant threw separate doors.
5. By myself I can't do much to improve trash collection in my neighborhood, but I can start a petition.
6. During the third week of his journey to the North Pole, Admiral Perry traveled further than in the first two weeks combined.
7. College-age listeners have the most different musical tastes of all age groups.

8. The old man shuttled slowly into the doctor's office and, at the nurse's direction, sat his battered hat on a table.
9. Since the new wing of the library has been open, many of its users have complained of feeling nauseous.
10. On most domestic flights, airlines no longer serve complementary meals.
11. If your unable to breath because of allergies, hay fever season is the worst time of the year.
12. After pouring over stacks of books, Ellen has identified all the experts she will site in her paper.
13. Some legislators could care less about how their votes for welfare reform will effect people's ability to feed and cloth themselves.
14. Most gamblers are libel to be more concerned with that allusive person called Lady Luck then they are with they're families or jobs.
15. Wearing a balky parka to hide what he would take, the thief strolled up one isle and down another, stealing without a tinge of guilty conscious, but when apprehended, he voraciously protested his innocents.

Exercise 51--Choosing Words with Appropriate Connotation

Circle the synonyms whose connotations best fit your positive, neutral, or negative response to the meaning of the following sentences. Be able to explain your choices. To learn how to choose words with appropriate connotation, see 25b in *The Ready Reference Handbook.*

a. In a (dark, dim, dusky, murky, gloomy) corner of the museum, Harold pulled Carol close and whispered that he loved her.
b. Ramon could provide only a little assistance to his parents, but he didn't need to offer an (apology, excuse, plea, alibi) for his actions. They (appreciated, valued, prized, treasured, cherished) whatever he did.
c. In a satiric gesture, the artist Ben Houston has painted a huge canvas (copying, imitating, aping, mimicking, mocking) Norman Rockwell's famous Thanksgiving painting.

d. Climbing the three-hundred-foot Devil's Lake cliffs without a rope was a (daring, daredevil, reckless, foolhardy) deed.

e. The principle stood in the school room door (gazing, glaring, staring, peering) at a teacher who, in turn, was (gazing, glaring, staring, peering) at his misbehaving students.

1. Suddenly, the teacher (took, seized, grasped, clutched, snatched, grabbed) a (scrawny, skinny, slender) child, the (cool, composed, collected, unruffled, nonchalant) instigator of the trouble, and (led, guided, piloted, steered, directed) him into the hall.
2. A group of conservative legislators have a (clever, cunning, ingenious, crafty, tricky) (plan, plot, scheme, project) to (block, prevent, check, frustrate) enforcement of the Endangered Species Act.
3. The (dirty, filthy, foul, nasty, squalid) room in which my uncle Merlin lived out the last months of his (solitary, lonely, forlorn, desolate) life was illuminated by one (bare, naked, uncovered) light bulb.
4. Intending to minimize expenses and maximize profits, the restaurant owners decorated the interior of their business with (imitation, fake, phony, artificial) flowers.
5. Folk art employs (common, ordinary, plain, familiar) household objects and transforms them into works of (surprising, unexpected, stupendous) power and beauty.

Exercise 52--Editing for Idiomatic Words

Edit the following sentences for the idiomatic use of words, especially prepositions. To learn to use words idiomatically, see 25f in *The Ready Reference Handbook.* Answers to lettered items appear in the back of this booklet. Example:

with
Please don't be angry ~~at~~ me; I'm only repeating what he said.
^

a. Creationists offer a novel solution for the extinction of the dinosaurs.

b. For me, cross-country skiing is preferable than down-hill skiing.

c. The mediator instructed the union and management to try and settle their differences in one all-night bargaining session.

d. Everyone tries to discourage me to major in journalism.

e. At the end of the State of the Union Address, Cheryl indicated that she differed from the President on several of his tax proposals.

1. It was painful for me to see him how he was after three weeks in the hospital.
2. I may have all the facts and a reasonable argument, but Larry never agrees to any of my opinions.
3. The frightened cat jumped off of the shed and dashed under a nearby bush.
4. Environmentalists are beginning to protest about the loss of valuable farmlands at the edges of large cities.
5. The adoptive parents came to the court accompanied with their foster child and their lawyer.
6. Because Ella was a distant cousin of the prosecuting attorney, the judge disqualified her to serve on the jury.
7. Before we finish raking the leaves, we intend on cleaning the gutters and downspouts.
8. Conservatives' opinions about the legitimate powers of the federal government are different than liberals' opinions.
9. When I drove from Paris to Rome, I was surprised to discover how similar Italian is with French.
10. Karen is not the type of a person who believes what everyone tells her.

Exercise 53--Choosing Specific and Concrete Words

Write a brief passage of two or three sentences about each of the following. Make your language as specific and concrete as possible. To learn to use specific and concrete words, see 26a and b in *The Ready Reference Handbook.*

1. A revealing description of someone you have observed closely. Example:

Whenever my family gets together for a holiday, my father spends the afternoon standing by the front door, jingling his pocket change to sound his impatience with unproductive socializing. Then, as if to count every wasted second that he could be spending at his office, he pulls the coins from his pocket and pours them from one hand to the other.

2. Revealing details about a place you know well

3. A malfunctioning device that you know well from experience

4. A social or environmental problem that you have observed first hand

5. A value, virtue, or standard that you wish more people possessed

Exercise 54--Creating Figurative Language: Metaphors and Similes

Use the following formula to create five metaphors or similes about the identified topics. Try several alternatives until you find one that is accurate, original, and vivid. Then rewrite to omit the formula so that the metaphor or simile stands alone as a complete sentence. If necessary, explain your comparison. To learn more about metaphors and similes, see 26c in *The Ready Reference Handbook*.

> If __(my subject)__ were __(choose from one of the following categories)__, it would/would not be __(make up a term to complete the formula)__.

a place	a piece of furniture	a smell	an article of clothing
a means of transportation	a movement	a food	a sound
a toy	a musical instrument	a road	a beverage
the weather	music	a work of art	a building
vegetation	a color	a shape	an animal
		a person	an object

1. Some part of your personality or your life. Example:

> If I were an item of food, I would be an open-faced avocado sandwich piled high with crisp green scallions and melted cheddar and mozzarella cheese, then sprinkled lightly with seasoned salt.
>
> I am a complex person of varied tastes and opinions, like an open-faced avocado sandwich piled high with crisp green scallions and melted cheddar and mozzarella cheese, then sprinkled lightly with seasoned salt.

--Wayne Deering, student

2. A person you know well or a feature of that person

3. A place you know well or a feature of that place

4. An event you have observed or a part of that event

5. A controversial subject you have opinions about

Exercise 55--Editing Clichés and Mixed Metaphors

Edit the following sentences to eliminate clichés and mixed metaphors. To learn about clichés and mixed metaphors, see 26d in *The Ready Reference Handbook.* Answers to lettered items appear in the back of this booklet. Example:

> **Bill and Darlene's friendship has ~~expanded to new depths~~** *deepened* **and will surely ~~span the test of time.~~** *endure.*

a. After a semester of absolute hell in which I beat my brains out working thirty hours a week and carrying five courses, I'm slowly but surely getting my act together again.

b. Two term papers due during finals week were the straw that broke the camel's back, made me a sadder but wiser student, and turned my life around.

c. Clumps of fireflies whizzed by as our car glided like an Olympic skater down the dark, deserted road.

d. It is so true that caught up in the hustle and bustle of big city life, residents of a large city like New York have no time to stop and smell the roses.

e. The question of whether to legalize drugs is a thorny, multi-sided issue.

1. Suddenly, after what seemed an endless blizzard of confusion, a spark jumped from her mind to mine and rekindled the flame of understanding.
2. A warm sea of familiar smiles flickered with appreciation and filled my heart with happiness.
3. The fat cat CEOs who make five or six times more than their employees don't see the big picture. If the wealth of our nation is not spread among all economic groups, it will be curtains for our way of life.
4. Jennie's deep insecurity is a facet of her personality that has started her on a chain of lies to her coworkers.

5. Underdeveloped nations that are harvesting their rain forests for temporary economic advantage should wake up and smell the coffee. By opening their markets to U.S. investment, they can come in out of the rain and gather under Uncle Sam's generous wing.

Exercise 56--Editing for Words Appropriate to Academic and Public Writing

Edit the following sentences to make them appropriate for serious academic and public writing. Eliminate slang, regionalisms, and nonstandard words. To learn to choose words that fit the occasion, see 27a and b in *The Ready Reference Handbook.* Answers to lettered items appear in the back of this booklet. Example:

Millions *now contracting*

~~So many millions~~ of young Americans are ~~getting~~ sexually transmitted diseases ~~these days!~~

a. The years following the stock market crash of 1929 were tough for most all Americans.

b. My low aptitude test scores almost messed up my chances for getting into college. I did get accepted at two state schools, though.

c. The writer Oscar Ramirez goes deep into the way in which American culture interacts with immigrant cultures and ends up different somehow.

d. Isn't it funny how slick politicians say they're all in favor of changing the way elections get paid for--until they get elected.

e. President Nixon really messed things up for himself and a bunch of his friends when he put tape recorders in his office at the White House.

1. Folks who preach integration assume that minorities and other ethnic groups will sort of blend into the majority culture.

2. The philosopher Albert Camus is always bringing up the point that people are free to choose their destinies, but he goes on to say that they've got to be responsible for their choices.

3. I can't stand the thought of graduating from college with only some low-wage, high-risk, no-benefits job staring me in the face.

4. I figure that someday soon someone's going to come up with a gimmick to fix up the ozone hole in the atmosphere over Antarctica.
5. This one famous biologist tells how we should just junk our notion of evolution as some kind of ladder. His theory revolves around the idea that evolution is like a bush with a bunch of branches sprouting every which way.

Exercise 57--Editing for Jargon and Pretentious or Misleading Words

Edit the following sentences to omit unnecessary jargon, pretentious words, "doublespeak," and euphemisms. More than one effective revision is possible. To learn to about jargon and pretentious or misleading words, see 27c and d in *The Ready Reference Handbook.* Answers to lettered items appear in the back of this booklet. Example:

talk to each other regularly about

The partners in the most enriching marriages ~~interact with each other on a~~

their relationship and how to make it successful.

~~regular basis in order to receive input and feedback necessary to sustain their relationship.~~

a. We regret to inform you that your brother expired at 4:13 pm.
b. Pickleworth's Restaurant offers a sumptuous dining experience of ample portions presented by gracious, attentive servers, resplendent in turn-of-the-century Victorian finery.
c. We are cognizant of the fact that in order to effect a successful outcome we must prioritize our endeavors according to their importance.
d. Substantial renovation of this domicile is essential to ensure its salability.
e. The 375 inhabitants of the DeVille Hotel were evacuated safely from the premises shortly after the inception of the conflagration. The only fatality was that of an elderly gentlemen who propelled himself from the roof of the structure due to panic on his behalf.

1. The majority of teenagers have had an intimate relationship by the time they are seventeen.
2. At this point in time, it is incumbent upon us to embark upon an employment search for an assistant instructional resource administrator responsible for disseminating innovative

instructional delivery systems to be utilized by all instructional personnel in this educational institution.

3. Resplendent in the brilliant rays of the early morning sun, the snow-draped evergreens sparkled in a luminous mantle of white.
4. As part of the downsizing process impacting the Rubber-Flex Corporation, Bentham's work was outsourced, and he was terminated.
5. A review of existing parameters suggests, firstly, a strong correlation between a reduction of the amount of required consumer cash flow and the increased outflow of merchandisable items.

Exercise 58--Editing for Sexist and Other Offensive Words

Edit the following sentences to omit sexist and other offensive words. More that one effective revision is possible. To learn how to avoid sexist and offensive words, see 27e in *The Ready Reference Handbook*. Answers to lettered items appear in the back of this booklet. Example:

The newly elected chairman of the board of trustees is ~~Mrs.~~ Christine Reilly~~, wife of Peter Reilly, president of the Firstline Corporation.~~

a. When our forefathers came to this country, most dreamed of more than economic security.
b. When a professional athlete signs his first professional sports contract, he may not know what to do with his instant wealth.
c. In most Western nations, colored people do not receive the kind of treatment that whites do.
d. All mankind, rich and poor alike, will eventually suffer if birth rates are not reduced.
e. For a handicapped person in a wheel chair, Elspeth is well conditioned and self-disciplined. She's even planning to enter this year's Boston Marathon.

1. In these days of heightened sensitivity, politicians are having trouble running against women.
2. A person doesn't become a nurse to be a speaker or writer, but some of her most important duties require that she use words clearly, accurately, and economically.

3. Whether a salesman, policeman, newsman, mailman, cleaning woman, or even a lowly stock boy, every worker expects a fair day's pay for a fair day's work.
4. The natives of South American countries don't all speak Spanish as their native language.
5. All of Barrington was shocked when it was discovered that the mayor had murdered his neighbor's wife.

Exercise 59--Editing for Wordiness

Edit the following sentences for wordiness. More than one effective revision is possible. To learn to identify wordy constructions, see Chapter 28 in *The Ready Reference Handbook.* Answers to lettered items appear in the back of this booklet. Example:

> *Gazing* **~~As I gazed~~ at the scattered contents of my apartment,** *I could see* **~~it was fairly obvious~~ that I had been burglarized, but ~~there was~~ something inside me** *refused* **~~refusing~~ to believe it.**

a. Some elderly people have a resistance to seeing themselves as old.

b. When the Christmas holidays come, I purchase all of my gift items from catalogs.

c. Bide-a-Wee Resort has a wide variety of campsites. There are pull-through sites with electricity and water, electricity-only sites, and primitive sites carved into bluffs.

d. Many different kinds of waste toxins can linger around in landfills, polluting the soil and ground water for dozens, even hundreds of years on end.

e. The position of an executive secretary falls more in the category of administrative assistant than mere clerk or typist.

1. In this pleasant garden is seen an amiable-looking old man who is dressed in a tattered tuxedo and is seated under a linden tree.
2. I see the people of the world as a whole divided into three specific groups.
3. Unfortunately, my brother had the misfortune of being wounded during the Gulf War.

4. Mayor Jenkins recently made an announcement saying that leaflets would be sent to all community members in the near future to come to get more citizen involvement going.
5. The natural decorations in Mammoth Cave include the flower-like gypsum crystals, which cover the walls. The formations, which are quite colorful, glow with the brilliant browns, oranges, and yellows of dissolved minerals.
6. When Helen redecorated her house, she had walls moved and repainted, new wall paper hung, and the woodwork stripped and revarnished. She did not stop until perfection was achieved.
7. Nick's parents impressed upon young Nick the fact that he was different from his playmates.
8. In my opinion, I think there is a definite need for more private enterprises to provide financial assistance to non-profit community organizations.
9. The room is perfectly square in size, and in the very center there is a small chandelier which hangs above a round table.
10. Our pontoon boat was fun to putter around in, but when we wanted to go water skiing, it was necessary to rent a more powerful boat.
11. The damage to the radiator was the cause of an impairment in the function of the cooling system.
12. When I reflect back upon it, I must confess a factual truth: my success was caused more by dumb luck than merit or skill.
13. The reason why unemployment figures in the United States are generally so low is because the Bureau of Labor Statistics does not count jobless people who have given up looking for work.
14. In the modern age of today, people have turned to hypnotists for help in the areas of quitting smoking, losing weight, and curing phobias. Who knows what uses we will make of hypnosis in the future to come.

15. I want to highlight the fact that my transition from a small-town high school to a large university atmosphere was a very challenging test. At first, faced with dozens of unfamiliar strangers in class and my dormitory, I saw my confidence dwindle down to almost nothing, and I was filled with feelings of self-doubt that I would ever successfully pass the test of being away from home for the first time in my life.

Exercise 60--Using Articles

In the following sentences, fill in the blanks with *a, an, the,* or an "X" when no article is appropriate. To learn to use articles, see 30a-d in *The Ready Reference Handbook.* Answers to lettered items appear in the back of this booklet. Example:

__X__ India is __the__ world's second most populous nation. __The__ most populous is, of course, __X__ China.

a. _____ jewelry is my wife's favorite gift.

b. _____ jewelry she prefers is made of _____ sterling silver.

c. _____ English looks simpler than _____ inflected language like _____ French.

d. _____ Korean language resembles _____ Japanese in grammatical structure, but it uses _____ different writing system known as _____ Hangul.

e. It seems that each culture has _____ different standard for _____ beauty.

1. _____ woman knocked on my door last night. _____ woman spoke _____ language I could not understand.

2. My supervisor gave me _____ time off to study for final exams, but _____ time I needed most was _____ time to sleep.

3. _____ game of _____ jai lai is played on _____ three-walled court called _____ fronton, using a hard rubber ball and _____ cesta, _____ curved wicker basket attached to _____ player's arm.

4. _____ tense moment when you first arrive in _____ new country is going through _____ customs.

5. _____ Himalayas are _____ home of _____ snow leopard.

Exercise 61--Editing Articles and Quantifiers

Edit the following sentences for errors in the use of articles, quantifiers, and nouns. If a sentence is correct, write "correct" after it. To learn to use articles and quantifiers, see Chapter 30 in *The Ready Reference Handbook.* Answers to lettered items appear in the back of this booklet. Example:

Street a
~~A street~~ crime is not ^ common problem in my country.

a. After hiking two more miles, we found a easy way down the mountain.

b. The territorial behavior is expressed by the humans and the animals alike.

c. Finally, the soccer is becoming popular game in the United States.

d. Every Friday evening I go out to eat with the several of my friends.

e. Although I'm not the musician, I enjoy the music very much, and the music I enjoy most is the jazz.

1. The United States is one of wealthiest nations in the world and has one of most liberal immigration policies, so no wonder the people from the less wealthy nations want to immigrate to the US.
2. After yesterday's snow storm, small boy with large shovel came to my door and said he would clean my walk or sell shovel to me.
3. *Things Fall Apart,* the novel by Nigerian writer Chinua Achebe, describes the life in African village.
4. Caste system in India and South Africa's apartheid are best examples of harmful systems of social classification.
5. Well-developed bi-lingual education programs help immigrants find a home in the strange country.
6. The Mandarin, spoken by two-thirds of the Chinese population, is one of the most important Chinese dialect.

7. Most of people living on my block were born in Philippines.

8. Coming from tropics, I am not used to a cold weather.

9. Whenever I fly, it seems, I lose some of my luggages.

10. A little girl standing ahead of me at the theater snack bar wanted some popcorn and a candy bar, but a woman, obviously her mother, told the girl that the popcorn was too salty and the candy bar too sweet and offered her an apple, instead.

Exercise 62--Editing for Correct Verb Forms

Edit the following sentences for the correct use of helping verbs, main verbs, modal verbs, and the passive voice. To learn to use correct verb forms, see 31a-d in *The Ready Reference Handbook*. See 13a3 for a list of irregular verb forms. Answers to lettered items appear in the back of this booklet. Example:

has -d

To attract foreign investment, my government ~~have~~ devalue its currency.

^ ^

a. By the time I receive my flu shot I am already having the flu twice this year.

b. When the hurricane struck, our car was sat under two huge palm trees.

c. Hasn't anyone ever tell you that cigars can be as deadly as cigarettes?

d. When handling HIV patients, you do not suppose to work with your bare hands.

e. We would have love to attend the party.

1. We might could go to Acapulco with Juan if we had a little more time to save our money.

2. We have not yet decide what to name our new puppy.

3. The name for Mexico is take from the Mexica, one of seven ancient tribes that once inhabit the interior of the country.

4. We have wrote a proposal to start an international honors club on campus.

5. After last night's drawing, we've tore up all our lottery tickets and swore never to buy another one.

6. Children who are beating when young often grow up to abuse their children.

7. Did you kept the reward you were giving for returning the missing wallet?

8. We were frozen last night while the furnace was off.

9. During his final pilgrimage, the prophet Muhammad said that he has fulfilled his mission by leaving behind "God's Book."

10. Because he is not a very introspective person, he has not reflect on the causes of his troubles but has instead blame everyone else.

11. After we have finish our final exams, let's go out and celebrate.

12. At the end of the party, we will drinking to one another's health and long life.

13. So much emphasis is place on beauty in our society that you would think we have nothing of value inside us.

14. I know what discrimination feel like; it has happen to my family.

15. America made up of immigrants from around the world; even Native Americans migrate across the Arctic ice sheet thousands of years ago.

Exercise 63--Choosing Verb Forms in Conditional Sentences

In each sentence, fill in the blank with the correct conditional form of the verb in parentheses. Include any necessary helping verbs. In some sentences, the base form of the verb is correct. To learn to use verbs in conditional sentences, see 31e in *The Ready Reference Handbook.* Answers to lettered items appear in the back of this booklet. Example:

If I were you, I *would not write* **that letter.**
(not + write)

a. Whenever I __________ a scratchiness in my throat, I know I'm catching a cold.
(feel)

b. If there __________ true social equality, workers would receive equal pay for equal work, whatever their gender.
(be)

c. I __________ for the job if I had proofread my application more carefully.
(choose [Use the passive voice.])

d. Barry will leave for the airport when he __________ packing.
(finish)

e. The defendant __________ to plead guilty if the judge had agreed to a sentence of probation.
(agree)

1. If the snow continues to fall at this rate, it __________ more than an hour to get to work.
(take)

2. If the tide were just a little higher, we __________ launch our boat.
(can)

3. Unless I begin losing weight now, I __________ into my wedding tuxedo.
(never + squeeze)

4. If the weather patterns over Japan __________ just slightly different, the United States would not have dropped the atomic bomb on Nagasaki.
(be)

5. If the committee has already voted to adjourn, we __________ our proposal for the next meeting.
(save)

Exercise 64--Editing Conditional Sentences

Edit the following conditional sentences for the correct use of helping verbs, main verbs, and modal verbs. To learn to write conditional sentences, see 31c in *The Ready Reference Handbook.* See 13a3 for a list of irregular verb forms. Answers to lettered items appear in the back of this booklet. Example:

were
If we ~~would~~ not ~~be~~ so busy, we might go to a movie.
^

a. You would have seen a spectacular meteor shower if you went for a walk with us.

b. If I leave my house by 6 o'clock I would arrive at your house by seven.

c. Ho would be a better musician if he would spend more time practicing.

d. If Carol was less outspoken, she would offend fewer people.

e. Whenever I am most absorbed by my work, the telephone will ring.

1. I would have recommended Ilyas for the job if he didn't withdraw his name from consideration.

2. When Dayani would try to save a file on his computer, he received an error message.

3. If Magda has enough money, she would travel all over the world.

4. When the volcano would erupt, the lava will probably flow down its north slope.

5. If Anna had mentioned her interest in Renaissance painters, we had invited her to go to the museum with us.

Exercise 65--Choosing Infinitives or Gerunds

In each sentence, fill in the blank with either the infinitive or the gerund form of the verb in parentheses. To learn to use infinitives and gerunds correctly, see 31f in *The Ready Reference Handbook.* Answers to lettered items appear in the back of this booklet. Example:

I dream of ___*living*___ (live) **deep in a forest of pine and fir; I would like you** ___*to join*___ (join) **me.**

a. All workers on the site are required __________ (wear) hard hats.

b. Teresa was beginning __________ (think) that no one was interested in __________ (buy) her handmade jewelry.

c. Nashunda advised her clients __________ (file) a suit and __________ (demand) a generous settlement.

d. Seldom do I feel like __________ (practice) the piano, but my father encourages me __________ (sit) down and __________ (begin).

e. Bernard walked next door and asked his neighbors __________ (stop) __________ (play) their stereo so loudly.

1. Arne appreciated __________ (win) a scholarship to a major university, but decided __________ (attend) a smaller school, instead.

2. The Johnsons persuaded a young couple __________ (buy) their house and agreed __________ (help) with the financing.

3. Daniel pretended not __________ (hear) the couple in the seat in front of him talking about __________ (get) a divorce.

4. I don't claim __________ (be) an expert on the weather, but I'm warning you not __________ (stand) under a tree during a thunderstorm.

5. Javier was excited about __________ (start) his new job, but he reminded himself __________ (behave) in a professional manner.

Exercise 66--Editing Infinitives and Gerunds

Edit the following sentences for the correct use of infinitives and gerunds. If a sentence is correct, write "correct" after it. To learn to use infinitives and gerunds correctly, see 31f in *The Ready Reference Handbook.* Answers to lettered items appear in the back of this booklet. Example:

> **I am used to ~~live~~ living in a hot climate, so summers in Arizona don't bother me.**

a. My family and I are planning going to the Grand Canyon next summer.

b. You can depend on me to help you in any way possible.

c. We are looking forward to see lions, elephants, and zebras in the wild game parks of Kenya.

d. I object to spending so much money for a car that I'm only going to drive back and forth to work.

e. After the way they embarrassed me, I refuse speaking to them any more.

1. Juan intends to finish building his deck by the end of September.

2. I suggest to postpone your mother's surgery until she is stronger.

3. Stop thinking of yourself so much and try thinking of others.

4. We expect the waiter serving us our food courteously and promptly.

5. When immigrants become citizens of the United States, they do not instantly stop to being Italian or Vietnamese.

Exercise 67--Completing Two-Word Verbs

In each sentence, fill in the blank with the correct preposition to complete the two-word verb. To learn to use verbs in conditional sentences, see 31g in *The Ready Reference Handbook.* Answers to lettered items appear in the back of this booklet. Example:

It's late. I'm going to turn _out_ the lights and go to bed.

a. Shut _____ the engine so that we don't run _____ of gas.

b. I was so angry that I tore _____ the letter and threw it _____ .

c. Timothy and Angela left an hour ago; we'll never catch _____ with them.

d. Please turn _____ your assignments by Friday afternoon at the latest.

e. When my best friends come home in the evenings, the first thing they do is turn _____ their stereo and turn _____ the volume so that all their neighbors can hear them.

1. Shabana was the kind of person who always looked _____ for her friends.
2. The next time you're in town, please drop _____ to see us.
3. Fill _____ this application and give it _____ to me when you're finished.
4. Look _____ this list and cross _____ any items we don't need.
5. When the desperate criminal would not give _____, the police had to break _____ the door to his house.

Exercise 68--Editing Omissions and Repetitions

In the following sentences, include necessary subjects and expletives; delete any repeated subjects, objects, adverbs, or conjunctions. To learn to edit for necessary and unnecessary words in English sentences, see 32a and b in *The Ready Reference Handbook.* Answers to lettered items appear in the back of this booklet. Example:

In November 1995, Lech Walesa ~~he~~ narrowly lost Poland's presidential election.

a. I know this is true because has happened to me.

b. In some parts of Saudi Arabia, ten years may pass there without rainfall.

c. The Amazon Valley of eastern Ecuador it constitutes about half the country's area.

d. Are many orchards and gardens in the Nile River valley.

e. Because all of Nigeria lies within the tropics, so there are only two seasons, wet and dry.

1. I don't intend to marry before am twenty-four.
2. Iraq, the land where the Tigris and Euphrates rivers flow there, was once known as Mesopotamia, "the land between the rivers."
3. My college education is being paid for by an uncle I worked for him after graduating from high school.
4. Bolivia is a landlocked country. Is surrounded by Brazil, Paraguay, Argentina, Chile, and Peru.
5. Ancient civilizations, including the Maya and Aztec, they flourished in Mexico centuries before the Spanish conquest in the 16th century.

Exercise 69--Editing Summarized Questions and Speech

Edit the following sentences to correct errors in summarized questions and speech. Consider word choice, word order, verb forms, and punctuation. If a sentence is correct, write "correct" after it. To learn to summarize questions and speech correctly, see 32c in *The Ready Reference Handbook.* Answers to lettered items appear in the back of this booklet. Example:

are

Ask the museum guide where ~~are~~ the mummies.
^

a. An old man sitting next to me on a park bench said that once he was wealthy and powerful.

b. In my environmental ethics class we spent a whole week debating should the federal government act to preserve wetlands.

c. When I called, Natalie told me she is getting dressed and will be ready in fifteen minutes.

d. After the plane had been in the air for an hour, Stephen nervously asked how long will it be before he arrives in Los Angeles?

e. Yesterday, my supervisor asked me would I like to attend this year's COMDEX computer convention in Las Vegas?

1. I replied that I will love to go, but I wondered to myself who else will be going.
2. Then she asked me did I intend to spend any time in the casinos while I am in Las Vegas?
3. I answered I may rent a car and drive out into the desert or visit Hoover Dam.
4. She wondered why don't I want to gamble?
5. And then I tell her go take a look at the size of my bank account!

Exercise 70--Editing -ing *and* -ed *Adjectives (Participles)*

Edit the following sentences for the appropriate use of present and past participles. If a sentence is correct, write "correct" after it. To learn to use participial adjectives correctly, see 32e2 in *The Ready Reference Handbook.* Answers to lettered items appear in the back of this booklet. Example:

I wasn't simply ~~annoying~~ *annoyed* **when my car wouldn't start; I was ~~enraging~~** *enraged***.**

a. We were pleased to see that the finished product turned out the way we had planned.
b. She thought he was the most fascinated person she had ever met.
c. Casey said she was not interesting in attending the urban planning lecture.
d. I had just finished eaten breakfast when the telephone rang.
e. After the police used riot control gas, the demonstrators were nauseating for several hours.

1. Were weren't surprised that she was hired; her training, character, and experience made her the most deserving candidate.
2. After the hurricane, the forest was filled with falling branches and uprooting trees.
3. A grown child should drink lots of milk because calcium is requiring for healthy bones.
4. At first I was confused by all the complicating instructions.
5. Defeating her most feared opponent was for Jan a satisfying, even exhilarating experience.

Exercise 71--Arranging Cumulative Adjectives and Placing Adverbs

Edit the following sentences for the correct arrangement of cumulative adjectives and the correct placement of adverbs. If a sentence is correct, write "correct" after it. To learn to arrange cumulative adjectives and place adverbs correctly, see 32e3 and 32e4 in *The Ready Reference Handbook.* Answers to lettered items appear in the back of this booklet. Example:

A heavyset old

~~An old heavyset~~ man pedaled slowly a bicycle down the narrow street.

^

a. Some kind of yellow thick slime was oozing rapidly from a pipe into the small stream.

b. In front of the tiny green cottage stood two tall pine trees, the boughs heavy with freshly fallen snow.

c. Waiters like to see Armand stroll through a restaurant door because he leaves always large tips.

d. When my rich aunt comes to visit, she brings often little gifts to remind us just how rich she is.

e. During the Vietnam War, several Buddhist devout monks burned themselves to death to protest the conflict.

1. Vincent invited his best four friends to visit him at his vacation new home.
2. I realized slowly that a dark tall man dressed in a woolen heavy coat was staring at me.
3. Dropping quickly his position as an impartial observer, Jason protested the harsh treatment of the six young protestors.
4. A brown handsome retriever picked up eagerly the stick and carried it back to his master.
5. When the roof of the burning building collapsed, a huge black cloud spread menacingly above the fire fighters.

Exercise 72--Editing Prepositions of Place and Time

Edit the following sentences for the correct prepositions of place and time. If a sentence is correct, write "correct" after it. To learn to use these prepositions correctly, see 32f in *The Ready Reference Handbook.* Answers to lettered items appear in the back of this booklet. Example:

at *at*

We agreed to meet ~~in~~ midnight ~~on~~ the corner of 42nd Street and Broadway.

a. In most American restaurants, smokers and non-smokers are seated at different areas.

b. In the 1990s, people in the United States seem to have grown more conservative.

c. When Edgar arrived to the airport, he discovered that his plane was three hours late.

d. I meet so many interesting people in work.

e. For four long blocks a suspicious person followed me in the other side of the street.

1. At August, we usually spend a week to the beach in New Jersey.

2. On the evening of December 24th, my parents are planning to celebrate their twenty-ninth wedding anniversary in the grand ballroom of the Newmark Hotel.

3. On the evening, after a long day at school, I'm usually too tired to do anything more than stay at my room and watch television.

4. When Jeffrey grinned, his friends laughed at him because he had a piece of food caught on his teeth.

5. Lee sat down on her desk and tapped her finger nervously at its surface, waiting for the call which was to come promptly on noon.

Punctuating

Exercise 73--Editing End Punctuation

Edit the following sentences to correct errors in the use of periods, question marks, and exclamation points. If a sentence is correct, write "correct" after it. To learn to use end punctuation correctly, see Chapter 33 in *The Ready Reference Handbook.* Answers to lettered items appear in the back of this booklet. Example:

"Man is condemned to be free." the French writer Jean-Paul Sartre declared ironically.

a. Because most of the Earth is covered in a liquid mantle, science writer Dava Sobel says a more appropriate name for our planet would be "Water".

b. Was Thomas Jefferson the first to declare that human beings have the right to "life, liberty, and the pursuit of happiness?"

c. Most Americans believe that the federal government has hidden proof of UFOs from the public (a surprising twenty-percent believe UFOs represent alien life forms.).

d. According to one medical professor, laughter has such powerful health benefits that if it were bottled "it would require FDA approval."

e. The Japanese fliers began their surprise attack on Pearl Harbor at 7:50 a.m. and concluded their devastating bombardment by 10 a.m..

1. Recognizing that a free society's greatest threat springs from the intolerance bred of certitude, Judge Learned Hand cautioned, "The spirit of liberty is the spirit which is not too sure that it is right . . ."

2. Within the next few years, N.A.S.A. will send unmanned missions to Mars to collect rocks from the surface of the planet and carry them back to Earth.

3. For a number of years now, Americans have been asking themselves what responsibility our government has for the well being of our nation's citizens?

4. Nutritional researchers have recently been asking themselves, "How much fat is contained in products advertised as being low in fat"?

5. I couldn't believe it! My first apartment! And in a fancy high-rise, no less! I was nearly breathless at the view of the city spread out twenty-four floors below!

Exercise 74--Commas: Punctuating Compounds and Introductory Words

In the following sentences, add commas before conjunctions that link the independent clauses of compound sentences and after introductory words. If a sentence does not require additional punctuation, write "correct" after it. To learn about commas with compounds and introductory words, see 34a and b in *The Ready Reference Handbook.* Answers to lettered items appear in the back of this booklet. Example:

During a lunar eclipse the moon sometimes has a reddish color.
^

a. The Eiffel Tower was erected for the Paris Exposition of 1889 and remained the tallest structure in the world until 1930.

b. To detect the presence of drugs researchers mix blood with genetically engineered antibodies.

c. When cirrus clouds form they are frequently a sign of changing weather.

d. Jeff's uncle has smoked cigarettes for forty years so he shouldn't be surprised at his frequent lung ailments.

e. The water in the upper Rhine River comes primarily from the melting snow of the Alps but downstream the primary source is winter rain.

1. Sweeping away the sawdust with a wave of his hand the carpenter measured the board for his next cut.

2. Hiking in the Adirondack Mountains and reading two or three novels are my vacation plans for this summer.

3. When we stepped into the lobby we were blinded by the bright lights and glittering celebrities.

4. Suddenly the thief leaped from the shadows and threatened the helpless couple with a large knife.
5. Helen Keller was born blind and deaf yet she graduated from college with honors and mastered several languages.
6. As I stared at the smoking ruins of my house I thought that I must be dreaming and that I'd soon wake up.
7. When Hernando Cortés landed in Mexico in 1518 and began his march inland he intended to colonize the land for Spain and save souls for the Catholic Church.
8. My poor study habits were bound to affect my grades sooner or later and they did last semester.
9. Through the Cumberland Gap ran the Wilderness Road to Tennessee and the American frontier.
10. We could go out for a pizza or if you're concerned about your waistline we could share my last granola bar.

Exercise 75--Commas: Punctuating Series, Adjectives, and Modifiers

In the following sentences, add commas within series, between coordinate adjectives, and surrounding nonessential modifiers. If a sentence does not require additional punctuation, write "correct" after it. To learn about commas with series, adjectives, and modifiers, see 34c, d, and e in *The Ready Reference Handbook.* Answers to lettered items appear in the back of this booklet. Example:

The planets farthest from the Sun are Saturn^ Uranus^ Neptune^ and Pluto.

a. The old grandfather clock struck the hour with a deep softly echoing chime.
b. Dyslexia a severe learning disorder may be caused by brain malfunction or environmental influences.
c. Anyone who knows anything about rock 'n' roll appreciates Chuck Berry's artistry.
d. Sharon didn't discover the burglary until she went into her bedroom where she found her jewelry box open and empty.

e. St. Augustine Jamestown and the Plymouth Colony were three of the earliest European settlements in North America.

1. Kurt Vonnegut's novel *Slaughterhouse-Five* is a favorite of many high school and college students.
2. One of the joys of cooking on an outdoor charcoal grill is hearing the sizzling smacking sound of the juices hitting the brightly glowing coals.
3. You can go to the quick oil change outlets which charge more than twenty dollars or change your oil yourself for five or six dollars depending on the make and model of your car.
4. The prehistoric Cro-Magnon people are considered superior to their Neanderthal contemporaries because the Neanderthals used few tools and left little art.
5. Animal researchers often put their test subjects in a box called a *stock* which is used to immobilize them during testing.
6. The three goals of the 1804 Lewis and Clark expedition through the Louisiana Purchase were to find a land route to the Pacific strengthen claims to the Oregon Territory and gather information about the Indians.
7. Cherie and Eric planned a vacation in South Dakota's Black Hills the location of Mt. Rushmore Wind Cave and the Crazy Horse Monument.
8. England's prehistoric Stonehenge monument is constructed of four circular series of stones surround by a broad shallow ditch. Gerald Hawkins a British astronomer has proposed that these stones were used as a gigantic astronomical instrument.
9. Women who owned just five percent of American businesses in the 1970s now own forty percent.
10. Political candidates who spend the most on advertising are usually the ones who are most successful on election day.

Exercise 76--Commas: Other Uses

In the following sentences, add commas with transitions, parenthetical remarks, contrasts, quotations, direct address, the words *yes* and *no,* interjections, titles, dates, place names, and addresses. If a sentence does not require additional punctuation, write "correct" after it. To learn these uses of the comma, see 34f, g, and h in *The Ready Reference Handbook.* Answers to lettered items appear in the back of this booklet. Example:

Confucius advised "Have no friends not equal to yourself."

a. The inmates of US prisons tend to be the poor and uneducated as you might imagine.

b. The wealthy and well educated also commit crimes but unlike poor criminals have the resources to avoid conviction and if convicted imprisonment.

c. Many English words come from the names of real people for example *boycott* and *lynch.*

d. The fabulous golden city of El Dorado was as historians recognize a figment of early Spanish explorers' imaginations.

e. "A soft answer turneth away wrath" the Bible reminds us.

1. The old saying "There's the rub" comes from an ancient bowling game and referred to something that hindered the movement of the ball.
2. On August 9 1945 the United States dropped its second atomic bomb on Nagasaki Japan.
3. Most people know Charles Lutwidge Dodgson as Lewis Carroll the author of *Alice in Wonderland;* however he was also an accomplished mathematician and photographer.
4. "The thing that impresses me most about America" remarked Edward, the Duke of Windsor "is the way parents obey their children."
5. The Grand Canyon is not only the longest but also the deepest canyon in the United States.
6. The auditorium of our new theater is large (with seating for four hundred people) but there is not nearly enough room backstage to store all our props.
7. Adolfo Chavez MD plans to feed undernourished Latin-American children artificially enriched "super tortillas."

8. Is it true Professor Crockett that Alfred Hitchcock's *Vertigo* is his best movie?

9. Cross-country skiing is the best exercise for burning calories don't you agree?

10. I too once believed recycling to be the solution to most problems of waste disposal.

Exercise 77--Commas: All Uses

Add necessary commas in the following sentences. If a sentence does not require additional punctuation, write "correct" after it. To learn about uses of the comma, see Chapter 34 in *The Ready Reference Handbook.* Answers to lettered items appear in the back of this booklet. Example:

> **The Middle Ages are often referred to as the "Dark Ages" but in fact they were a time of great learning and intellectual development.**

a. Ralph reached for his pocket calculator which he carried everywhere and quickly added up the long list of figures.

b. The Luddites were early 19th century weavers who wrecked their looms because they believed the machinery responsible for their low wages and unemployment.

c. Francis Bacon said "Some books are to be tasted others to be swallowed and some few to be chewed and digested."

d. Des Moines Iowa the state capital was founded in 1843 and originally called Fort Des Moines.

e. Some of the most intricately designed oriental rugs actually come from Kurdistan a region of northern Iraq and southern Turkey.

1. Although the Sargasso Sea is filled with seaweed it is in reality a great oceanic desert with the lowest amount of life in any sea water.

2. On June 8 1996 after taking classes for eleven years my father earned his bachelor's degree.

3. Many ancient diseases such as the plague leprosy and tuberculosis still have not been eradicated.

4. "Hello Dr. Melnick" Melanie said. "I have an appointment with you for May 12th that I'll have to reschedule."

5. After Marco Polo returned to Venice from Asia he was imprisoned during a war with Genoa and used his imprisonment to write the story of his travels.
6. The Americans lost the Battle of Bunker Hill (actually fought nearby at Breed's Hill) but although defeated they earned a moral victory by inflicting heavy casualties on the British.
7. After a cool rainy spring and a warm sunny summer autumn brought a blaze of color to the maple ash and oak trees behind our house.
8. Unsure of what she should say but certain that she had to say something Jenny rose to speak.
9. When I was a child my father never lost an opportunity to quote me his favorite proverb "Dig the well before you are thirsty."
10. Ginnie has never been able to finish a marathon; nevertheless after a summer of intense training she is ready to try again.

Exercise 78--Editing for Missing and Misused Commas

Add necessary commas and delete unnecessary commas in the following sentences. If a sentence requires no changes, write "correct" after it. To learn the correct uses of the comma, see Chapter 34 in *The Ready Reference Handbook*. Answers to lettered items appear in the back of this booklet. Example:

> **Whenever cold weather threatens the PADS program provides the homeless with a warm place to sleep, and a hot meal.**

a. Most people associate bagpipes with Scotland but, they originated in Greece and Asia.

b. If the "big bang" theory is correct the universe is about 10 billion years old.

c. According to the Catholic doctrine of papal infallibility, the Pope is an imperfect human being but he cannot lead the church into religious error.

d. Air pollution is severe in Albuquerque, because the city is located in a broad shallow valley.

e. To challenge someone in authority, who disagrees with me, is not easy to do.

1. "Will you please give me directions?", asked a well dressed, elderly woman.

2. The theme of Sophocles' tragedy *Antigone*, is that no one, not even a king, has all the answers, or the right to do whatever he wishes.
3. The most recent congressional proposal, which has little chance of passage, would deny federal funding to museums that exhibit morally controversial art.
4. During high school most adolescents struggle to accept themselves, and abandon their naive dream of being someone they are not.
5. Jamestown, Virginia was the first successful English colony in America, although, it nearly failed because of disease, hunger, and Indian attacks.
6. Our landlord raised our rent twenty dollars a month, however, he told us, that he would provide a generous decorating allowance.
7. The night shift staff, at the nursing home, never told us of our grandmother's sudden illness, and the day staff weren't aware that we hadn't been informed.
8. Contradicting many of its stereotypes, Borneo is not only rich in natural resources, but also complex in its history.
9. Construction on the Alaskan Highway was begun in April, 1942, to link remote, Alaskan military bases with the lower forty-eight states.
10. We spent the evening staring out the window of the hotel lobby, watching the pedestrians, as they hurried by in a driving rain.
11. The counsellor discussed many things with my brother and me, such as, our feelings about our parents' divorce, our attitudes towards their new spouses and our relations with each other.
12. The lesson of my mother's life is, that as long as a person has good character, skill and confidence he or she can succeed in life.
13. Mecca, the holiest city of the Muslim faith depends heavily upon pilgrims for its commerce.
14. The most important qualifications for a flight attendant are, good strength and balance, the patience of Job, and an ability to tolerate whining crabby people.

15. The science of silviculture studies the relationship of a forest to its environment, and the effects of planting, pruning, and harvesting on the forest.

Exercise 79--Punctuating with Commas and Semicolons

Punctuate the following sentences with commas and semicolons. If a sentence is correct, write "correct" after it. To learn to use semicolons, see Chapter 35 in *The Ready Reference Handbook.* Answers to lettered items appear in the back of this booklet. Example:

> **Talent consists of natural ability and skill ; genius , however , is a kind of compulsion , even a touch of madness.**

a. We judge ourselves by what we feel capable of doing while others judge us by what we have already done.

--Henry Wadsworth Longfellow

b. One never notices what has been done one can only see what remains to be done.

--Marie Curie

c. A fanatic is one who can't change his mind and won't change the subject.

--Winston Churchill

d. Books are good enough in their own way but they are a mighty bloodless substitute for life.

--Robert Louis Stevenson

e. Think before you speak is criticism's motto speak before you think is creation's.

--E. M. Forster

1. Advice is what we ask for when we already know the answer but wish we didn't.

--Erica Jong

2. When angry count ten before you speak if very angry an hundred.

--Thomas Jefferson

3. According to the philosopher Aristotle the roots of education are often bitter however its fruits are almost always sweet.

4. I believe that every right implies a responsibility every opportunity an obligation every possession a duty.

--John D. Rockefeller, Jr.

5. The buyer needs a hundred eyes the seller not one.

--George Herbert

Exercise 80--Editing Commas and Semicolons

Edit the following sentences for the misuse of commas and semicolons. If a sentence is correct, write "correct" after it. To learn to use semicolons, see Chapter 35 in *The Ready Reference Handbook*. Answers to lettered items appear in the back of this booklet. Example:

When my sister came home from the Army on her first leave, everyone in our family was thrilled; especially my mother.

a. People with heart disease are strongly cautioned to control their anger; instead of venting their emotions and risking a heart attack.

b. Vince pulled into the gas station for a fill-up; and as he stood at the pump, his eyes fell on the huge dent in his rear fender.

c. The contest for energy resources is now the primary cause of international conflicts; in the near future, however, the lack of safe drinking water will increasingly cause strife between thirsty nations.

d. According to the Center on Addiction and Substance Abuse, women get drunk more quickly than men; become addicted to drugs more quickly; and develop substance-abuse illnesses more quickly.

e. The old log cabin stood five feet from the ground; on a stone foundation; its log steps leading up to an open doorway.

1. The U.S. Justice Department reports that three out of every one hundred Americans are under correctional supervision; and that since 1980, the number has nearly tripled.
2. Neighbors are more than people who live next door, they are people who will watch your house when you're away, people to enjoy a backyard cookout with, people to chat with after a long day at work.
3. Scientists have recently discovered that a person's happiness has a "set point"; a biologically determined level to which it always returns.
4. Since earliest times, people have tried to choose the sex of their children, indulging in macabre rituals; even selling their souls to imaginary devils.
5. Child labor is increasing in the U.S. for several reasons; the growth of service work, the increasing number of part-time jobs, and the demand for a more flexible work force.
6. Richard Rodriguez explains America's cultural evolution when he asserts; "In the blending [of different ethnic cultures], we became what our parents have never been, and we carried America one revolution further."
7. Aid to poor children in America is becoming more difficult to provide because state welfare funding has declined; and because federal welfare legislation is now more restrictive.
8. Nearly half of all Americans believe in the existence of unidentified flying objects (UFOs), however, only twelve percent say they have actually seen such objects.
9. Saturated fat is more likely than other types of fat to raise blood cholesterol; which has been linked to increased risk of heart disease.
10. When Debbie Burton signed her first professional basketball contract, she received a salary of one million dollars per year; plus part ownership of her team.

Exercise 81--Punctuating with Commas, Semicolons, and Colons

Punctuate the following sentences with commas, semicolons, and colons. If a sentence is correct, write "correct" after it. To learn to use colons, see Chapter 36 in *The Ready Reference Handbook.* Answers to lettered items appear in the back of this booklet. Example:

;
A book is a mirror when a monkey looks in no apostle can look out.
^ ^

--George Christoph Lichtenberg

a. There are only two families in the world, as grandmother used to say the haves and the have-nots.

--Miguel De Cervantes

b. Pay attention to your enemies for they are the first to discover your mistakes.

--Antisthenes

c. All art is autobiographical the pearl is the oyster's autobiography.

--Federico Fellini

d. Calamities are of two kinds misfortune to ourselves and good fortune to others.

--Ambrose Bierce

e. Samuel Johnson offers writers surprising advice "Read over your compositions and wherever you meet with a passage that you think is particularly fine strike it out."

1. It's a recession when your neighbor loses his job it's a depression when you lose your own.

--Harry S Truman

2. For the most part Americans are an intemperate people we eat too much when we can drink too much indulge our senses too much.

--John Steinbeck

3. That is the essence of science ask an impertinent question and you are on your way to a pertinent answer.

--Jacob Bronowski

4. We hold these truths to be self-evident that all men are created equal that they are endowed by their creator with inherent and inalienable rights that among these are life liberty and the pursuit of happiness.

--Thomas Jefferson

5. There is a homely adage which runs "Speak softly and carry a big stick you will go far."

--Theodore Roosevelt

Exercise 82--Editing Commas, Semicolons, and Colons

Edit the following sentences for the misuse of commas, semicolons, and colons. If a sentence is correct, write "correct" after it. To learn to use colons, see Chapter 36 in *The Ready Reference Handbook*. Answers to lettered items appear in the back of this booklet. Example:

The poet Amy Lowell pointed out the key difference between young people and their elders; "Youth condemns, maturity condones."

a. Barbara's allergies make her so sensitive to food that she can eat only one kind; beige food.

b. Some of the most dangerous sports include: climbing, cycling, swimming, skiing, and football.

c. Where is it stated in the Constitution that: all Americans are guaranteed happiness and a life as comfortable as the next person's?

d. The best description of big-city life is the definition of *pluralism:* "a condition of society in which numerous ethnic, religious, or cultural groups coexist."

e. Victims of AIDS suffer a variety of symptoms, such as: coughing, shortness of breath, skin lesions that do not heal, seizures, cramps, diarrhea, and memory loss.

1. The secret to the tastiest fajitas consists of: marinating the meat in a spicy pepper sauce for two hours and grilling the meat with only the freshest peppers and onions.

2. Smoking appeals to the young primarily for social reasons, it provides a badge of daring and independence.

3. Many bakery goods are filled with artery clogging fat; for example: cinnamon rolls, brownies, cheesecake, and most muffins.
4. After Scrooge received his three ghostly visitors, he began doing good deeds for the first time in his life; such as: buying a goose for the Cratchit family and donating large sums of money to charity.
5. As the result my carelessness and lack of practice, my great ski adventure left me with: two broken clavicles, a cracked rib, a strained back, and a pulled hamstring muscle.

Exercise 83--Editing Apostrophes

Edit the following sentences to correct errors in the use of apostrophes. If a sentence is correct, write "correct" after it. To learn to use apostrophes, see Chapter 36 in *The Ready Reference Handbook*. Answers to lettered items appear in the back of this booklet. Example:

> Lets face it: as we grow older, our parents values inevitably become our's.

a. Greshams Law refers to peoples preference for spending overvalued currency and hoarding undervalued currency.
b. Stacys sister works as a field investigator in the FBIs Dallas office.
c. The summers of 88 and 89 were Americas driest since the dust-bowl years of the Great Depression.
d. The childrens delighted cries echoed from the playground.
e. The Old Mill Inn's best menu items are fresh catfish, steak, and taco's.

1. If old Jack Frosts nipping at your nose, fingers, and toes, thats because theyre unprotected against winter weather.
2. You're praise for Bostons professional hockey team shows that you do'nt know much about the sport.

3. After winning the jury's attention, the lawyer methodically exposed the flaws in her opponent's case.
4. Our towns landfill sends its odors our way whenever a south wind blows.
5. The communities' new recreation center was funded by a local citizens winning lottery ticket.
6. The Board of Supervisor's report lists their activities for the past year and presents next years budget.
7. The Golden Rule commands that we be concerned with others well being besides our own.
8. As Beth left the airplane, she picked up someone elses suitcase instead of hers.
9. Americans, who's tax rates are among the lowest in the world, complain that no ones taxes are as large as their's.
10. Tennessee Williams' play *A Streetcar Named Desire* tells of Blanche DuBois and Stanley Kowalski's desperate struggle for power.

Exercise 84--Punctuating Quotations

Punctuate the following sentences to supply missing quotation marks, periods, commas, colons, semicolons, question marks, and exclamation points where necessary. If a sentence does not require additional punctuation, write "correct" after it. To learn about quotation marks, see Chapter 38 in *The Ready Reference Handbook.* Answers to lettered items appear in the back of this booklet. Example:

What cynical politician said "If you want to get along, go along"?

a. When the patient awoke, he asked the surgeon Did everything go okay
b. The reward of a thing well done said Ralph Waldo Emerson is to have done it
c. My supervisor has just recommended that I shorten my report by two pages.
d. The ancient philosopher Quintilian defined ambition as the parent of virtue.
e. Are you familiar with Gwendolyn Brooks's poem We Real Cool

1. Kevin burst through the door shouting excitedly Don't start the party without me

2. You don't write because you want to say something observed F. Scott Fitzgerald; you write because you've got something to say.

3. The students asked whether they could read a scene from Romeo and Juliet for their class presentation.

4. The old saying hear no evil, see no evil, speak no evil is the prescription for an uninteresting life

5. Mathematicians refer playfully to what they call a random walk: a series of randomly determined movements

6. What does Hamlet mean when he says to himself To be or not to be: that is the question

7. When life's obstacles seem insurmountable, remember Aesop's advice The gods help them that help themselves

8. When printers refer to a gutter, they aren't referring to streets but to the white space between the facing pages of a book.

9. Three of the best American short stories are Rip Van Winkle, Young Goodman Brown, and The Fall of the House of Usher

10. Every time I call to complain sighed Eric I get the same message We're sorry. No one can take your call right now

Exercise 85--Editing Quotations

Make necessary punctuation changes in the following sentences. Consider quotation marks, periods, commas, colons, semicolons, question marks, and exclamation points. To learn about editing quotations, see Chapter 38 in *The Ready Reference Handbook*. Answers to lettered items appear in the back of this booklet. Example:

The nervous man cried that "the bus he was waiting for was always late!"

a. The beggar asked Jeff whether he had any "spare change."

b. "Are these bags yours or his," the ticket agent asked?

c. The funeral director indicated that "cremation was not as expensive as burial."

d. Midwives provide assistance with what is called ‘natural childbirth,’ a process involving no anaesthesia or surgery.

e. “All rise”, the bailiff called out to the courtroom.

1. “If the question does not apply to you” said the personnel officer, “write “Does Not Apply” in the blank.”
2. What American writer said, “The trouble with the profit system has always been that it was highly unprofitable to most people?”
3. “A horse! A horse! My kingdom for a horse!”, cried the desperate king.
4. Television has been called a “vast cultural wasteland;” nevertheless, its educational potential is great.
5. Whenever he makes a mistake, Harry gives the same excuse, “To err is human; to forgive divine.”

Exercise 86--Editing the Dash, Parentheses, Brackets, the Ellipsis, and the Slash

Edit the following sentences to correct errors in the use of the dash, parentheses, brackets, the ellipsis, and the slash. If a sentence is correct, write “correct” after it. To learn to use these punctuation marks correctly, see Chapter 39 in *The Ready Reference Handbook.* Answers to lettered items appear in the back of this booklet. Example:

As Thomas Paine observed, “Government, even in its best state, is but a necessary evil . . .”

a. Ernest Wynder identifies the paradoxical goal of modern medicine as helping “. . . people die young as late in life as possible.”

b. With Shakespeare, I believe that fate is more than the sum of our choices: “There’s a divinity that shapes our ends, / Rough-hew them how we will.”

c. The aurora australis--the southern lights--glow as brightly and dynamically in the southern hemisphere as the aurora borealis glow in the northern hemisphere.

d. Reducing welfare payments to poor families, without providing funds for job creation, job training, and day care, will do nothing to reduce the number of poor people.

e. The terrain of China rises (almost like steps) from the lowlands of the east coast to the high mountains of the west.

1. The most common color of these celestial lights is the green of ionized (or excited) oxygen atoms.
2. Kosher foods include fish (with fins and scales but exclude shellfish and eels).
3. Astronomers now estimate that the universe contains fifty billion galaxies--forty billion more than previously believed, and hundreds of billions of stars with planetary systems.
4. Criminologist Sanford James cautions, "Although Americans now favor it [capital punishment] overwhelmingly, . . . public opinion may change as executions increase."
5. Japanese forests--which cover nearly seventy percent of the country--are largely inaccessible to efficient logging operations.

Exercise 87--Editing Capital Letters

Edit the following sentences to correct errors in capitalization. If a sentence is correct, write "correct" after it. To learn to capitalize correctly, see Chapter 40 in *The Ready Reference Handbook.* Answers to lettered items appear in the back of this booklet. Example:

must not weaken
The federal government ~~MUST NOT WEAKEN~~ the environmental laws that guarantee clean air and water.

a. The small country town where I grew up was so small that its Downtown consisted of only a General Store and a tiny Post Office.

b. Zachary Taylor, twelfth President of the United States, died of cholera after serving for less than one year.

c. Many hispanics would prefer to be referred to as latinos or latinas.

d. My Aunt and Uncle have invited me to live with them if I attend school near their home.

e. This evening's speech on anti-drug legislation will be given by attorney general Janet Reno.

1. The Great Plains begin west of Canada's Laurentian Highlands and run to the eastern edge of the Rocky Mountains.
2. I'll wait until the Spring semester to take an introductory spanish course and the required biology course.
3. The Art Institute of Chicago has just concluded a large exhibition of paintings by Claude Monet, the great French Impressionist.
4. The headwaters of the Colorado river are located on the western border of Rocky Mountain national park.
5. Most young people today have grown a little tired hearing their parents reminisce about how great everything was back in the Hippie Era of the Sixties.

Exercise 88--Editing Italics/Underlining

Edit the following sentences to correct errors in the use of italics. Underline to signal italics. If a sentence is correct, write "correct" after it. To learn to use italics or underlining correctly, see Chapter 41 in *The Ready Reference Handbook.* Answers to lettered items appear in the back of this booklet. Example:

John Milton's long poem Paradise Lost tells the story of Adam and Eve's temptation, fall, and expulsion from the Garden of Eden.

a. Willa Cather's most popular novel is probably "My Antonia."

b. The Supreme Court's decision in Gideon v. Wainwright gave the right to legal counsel to all accused persons.

c. NASA's Pathfinder spacecraft is scheduled to land on Mars on July 4, 1997.

d. The conductor directed the violin section to play *con brio,* with fire and vivacity.

e. The first three books of the *New Testament--Matthew, Mark, and Luke*--are believed to be based on an earlier account of Jesus's life.

1. A recent story in *The New York Times* describes the extent to which workers are subject to on-the-job surveillance.
2. When most people refer to Charles Darwin's "The Origin of Species," they add an extra "the," making the book's title "The Origin of the Species."
3. The old *hacienda* at the edge of the Dallas business district has been transformed into a trendy restaurant.
4. The boxer struck his dazed opponent in a frenzy of blows--*again* and *again, harder* and *harder*--until he fell unconscious to the canvas.
5. Words like *neither* and *leisure* are exceptions to the *i* before *e* spelling rule.

Exercise 89--Editing Abbreviations

Edit the following sentences to correct errors in the use of abbreviations. If a sentence is correct, write "correct" after it. To learn to abbreviate correctly, see Chapter 42 in *The Ready Reference Handbook.* Answers to lettered items appear in the back of this booklet. Example:

birthday *Monday* *January.*
Martin Luther King's ~~b'day~~ is celebrated on the third ~~Mon.~~ of every ~~Jan.~~
^ ^ ^

a. NASA's *Clementine* spacecraft has used radar to locate ice in a giant lunar volcano twice the size of Puerto Rico and higher than Mount Everest.

b. According to Dr. Herman Tyroler, PhD, heart disease is no longer an illness primarily afflicting the affluent.

c. Returning from a night reconnaissance following the Battle of Chancellorsville, Gen. Jackson was wounded by some of his own men, who mistook him for the enemy.

d. One of the most famous photographs of World War II shows Gen. Douglas MacArthur wading ashore upon his return to the Philippines.

e. Computers that will process video signals should have at least one or two gigabytes of memory.

1. Cleopatra and her younger brother became joint rulers of Egypt in BC 51.
2. The eruption of Mount Vesuvius in AD 79 destroyed the nearby cities of Herculaneum, Pompeii, and Stabiae.
3. The Nat'l. Park Serv. and the Bur. of Land Mgt. are raising entry fees for national parks and wilderness areas.
4. Anyone intending to go to law school will benefit by taking poli. sci., soc., and pscyh. electives.
5. Greek gods and goddesses, e.g., Zeus and Hera, have flaws that reflect those of their human creators.

Exercise 90--Editing Numbers

Edit the following sentences to correct errors in the use of numbers. If a sentence is correct, write "correct" after it. To learn when to write numbers as words or figures, see Chapter 43 in *The Ready Reference Handbook.* Answers to lettered items appear in the back of this booklet. Example:

seven *2.1 million*
In 1896, only ~~7~~ ^ percent of the United States ~~2,100,000~~ ^ miles of roads were paved.

a. The most prolific builder of ancient Egyptian temples was probably King Ramses the 2nd.

b. A Chia bust of the late Jerry Garcia of the Grateful Dead rock group, already seeded to grow green hair, sells for twenty-one dollars, ninety-five cents.

c. Montana has recently imposed a seventy-five mph speed limit on its highways.

d. On a clear night, the average number of stars visible from an American suburb is 250; from the wilderness, the average is 2,500.

e. A small Swedish postage stamp has just been sold at auction for more than two million dollars.

1. 3,054 inmates were on the Death Rows of United States prisons at the beginning of 1996.

2. Of these condemned prisoners, 48 were women, the youngest was 18, and the oldest was 80.

3. During the middle of the 14th century, the Black Death, or bubonic plague, killed off from 25 to 50 percent of the European population.

4. Ancient Rome was attacked and destroyed by the Visigoths in AD 410.

5. Nearly 1/3 of all American employees' e-mail is read by their supervisors.

6. A recent survey indicated that eighty-two percent of Americans believe that we "buy and consume far more than we need."

7. Our Fourth of July vacation begins precisely at four-thirty p.m. tomorrow when I finish work.

8. In the United States, the ratio of those who die from tobacco-related illness to those who are murdered is 17:1.

9. Last year our company sold twenty-six two-seater airplanes.

10. Between 1969 and 1990, the average travel time for U.S. commuters dropped from twenty-two to 19.7 minutes, while average commuting distances increased from 9.4 to over ten miles.

Exercise 91--Editing Hyphens

Edit the following sentences to correct errors in the use of the hyphen. If a sentence is correct, write "correct" after it. To learn to use hyphens, see Chapter 44 in *The Ready Reference Handbook*. Answers to lettered items appear in the back of this booklet. Example:

Into the clear night sky ascended the space-ship on its four year mission to Mars.

a. The highway overpass cave-in was caused by a moderately severe earthquake.

b. When a reward was offered for information about the escaped prisoners, the police switchboard was flooded with calls.

c. One problem with modern housing developments is that street layout prevents the formation of genuine neighborhoods.

d. The "either/or" fallacy treats a many sided issue as if it had only two sides.

e. Seated in front of me at the theater last night was a well known television actor.

1. The economic consequences of computer networking will be as far-reaching as the process of electrification in the early twentieth century.

2. The quickly-moving storm dropped only four or five inches of snow, but the strong winds blew up four and five foot drifts.

3. Corrine succeeded in her job interview in part because she projected great self assurance.

4. Thirty three percent of Americans say they would like to spend more time alone.

5. During Christmas break, we're going mountain-climbing in the South-west.

Exercise 92--Editing Spelling

Edit the following sentences to correct common spelling errors. To learn tips and rules for correct spelling, see Chapter 45 in *The Ready Reference Handbook.* Answers to all items appear in the back of this booklet, accompanied by labels indicating the types of errors. Use these labels to identify the spelling rules or tips you need to study. Example:

> Parallel
> **~~Paralel~~ parking is a difficult driving skill for most people to learn.**

a. When I was young, my father was transfered frequently, and so we moved alot. That was alright with me because I was able to see the world for free.

b. I've been writting poetry since the begining of my sophomore year of high school.

c. A cite for the new sports arena has just been choosen. Planing for the new arena was begun a year and a half ago.

d. When I don't make a sale, I don't get payed, and lately I've been loosing lots of money.

e. Niether of my roomates will be liveing with me next semester; basicly, we were incompatable.

f. The forward to a book will help a responsable, efficeint researcher determine wheather the book is worth reading.

g. You may not reconize me when you see me because I now weigh less than I did when I graduated from grammer school. It was an exersise program that helped the most, that and staying as far as possable from the campus dinning room.

h. Have I told you about Dr. Alter, a history proffessor I had last semester? She is definitly the best teacher I've had.

i. My step-father grows the best tomatos I've ever eaten.

j. In 45 BC the Romans began the practice of adding an extra day to Febuary to harmenize the calender with the soler year.

k. Citys such as New York and Los Angeles contain many economicly healthy immigrant communitys.

l. Overweight consumers shouldn't be decieved by ads promising weight loss without calerie-cutting.

m. Michigan and New York are slowly becomming fameous for the quality of the wines produced there.

n. The wether along the California coast can be very changable.

o. Goverment lobbists have prevented the passage of much neccessary legislation.

Research

Exercise 93--Writing Source Citations (Bibliography)

Write a complete, correctly formatted bibliographic citation for each of the following sources. Use an appropriate citation style illustrated in *The Ready Reference Handbook:* the Modern Language Association (see MLA sample citations, 52b) or the American Psychological Association (see APA sample citations, 54c). Answers to lettered items appear in the back of this booklet.

a. A book.

Author: Dyan Zaslowsky
Title: These American Lands: Parks, Wilderness, and the Public Lands
Publication information: Holt and Company, New York, 1986

b. A periodical.

Author: J. Mark Morgan
Title: Resources, Recreationists, and Revenues: A Policy Dilemma for Today's State Park Systems
Periodical title: Environmental Ethics
Publication information: volume 18, number 3, Fall 1996
Page numbers of the article: 279-291

1. A newspaper article.

Author: Betsy Wade
Title: Finding Space in U.S. Parks
Newspaper: New York Times
Publication information: volume 145, July 28, 1996
Location of the article: Section 2, page 4 (Late Edition)

2. A book with two authors.

Authors: James I Weir and Anna K. Lipton
Title: Seeing Nature Whole
Publication information: EcoSource Publications, San Francisco, 1996

3. A periodical article reprinted in a book-length anthology:

Author: Wangari Maathai
Article title: Foresters Without Diplomas
Original periodical title: Ms. Magazine
Original publication information: March/April, 1991.
Reprint source: Being in the World
Editors: Scott H. Slovic and Terrell F. Dixon
Publication information: Macmillan Publishing Company, New York, 1993
Page numbers of the article: 694-698

Exercise 94--Avoiding Plagiarism

Decide whether the following uses of original source materials represent fair use or plagiarism. If an item is fair use, write "fair use" after it. Revise plagiarized examples so that they borrow materials fairly and document them appropriately according to the MLA (see 51a and b) or APA (see 54a) citation formats. More than one correct revision is possible for each plagiarized example. To learn how to use source materials fairly and avoid plagiarism, see 50d in *The Ready Reference Handbook.* Answers to lettered items appear in the back of this booklet.

a. *An original source:* Arches [National Park] is home to the largest collection of natural sandstone arches in the world, some 2,000 in all. Despite its barren, otherworldly appearance, the land is coated by a fragile crust upon which an ancient forest of fungi, bacteria, and moss grow barely an inch tall. Wildlife in the park ecosystem, from insects to deer, has evolved to graze and extract nutrients from the Lilliputian canopy. Although these plant communities have endured scorching sun and erratic rain-fall for millennia, they are highly vulnerable to the softest soles of hiking boots.
(Todd Wilkinson, "Crowd Control," *National Parks,* July-August, 1995, p. 37)

Fair use or plagiarism? According to Todd Wilkinson, such natural environments as Arches National Park contain fragile plant systems that tolerate harsh weather and consumption by insects and animals, but they are "highly vulnerable" to human use ("Crowd Control" 37).

b. *An original source:* Many of the lesser-known [national] parks are as breathtaking as, say, a Yellowstone or an Acadia, with a fraction of their "people pollution." In these underappreciated jewels of the America's natural heritage, visitors will find lush forests, desert landscapes, massive gorges, fields of wildflowers, and natural lakes. Wildlife includes bears, mountain lions, foxes, bighorn sheep, bison, deer, and eagles.
("Unsung Splendor," *Audubon,* July-August, 1996, p.76)

Fair use or plagiarism? The United States national park system contains many underappreciated jewels, seldom-visited parks with all the varied landscapes and wildlife found in well-known parks such as Yellowstone or Acadia but almost none of the people pollution ("Unsung Splendor" 76).

1. *An original source:* South Dakota's Wind Cave National Park, a less-traveled alternative to Mount Rushmore, consists of two disparate worlds. Above ground, a rolling land of grasses--blue grama, wheatgrass, and little bluestem--looks much as it might have when the first settlers arrived. A meeting ground of species, it nourishes the elm and burr oak of the eastern forests as well as the Southwest's yucca and cactus and the Mountain West's ponderosa pine and juniper--and it draws a diverse mix of wildlife, including bison, elk, pronghorn, and prairie dogs.

   The alternative landscape stretches for at least seventy-eight miles below ground; explorers add more mileage every month. One of the world's oldest caves, it is decorated with intricate formations millions of years old. Over the millennia, water seeped through the limestone, molding a complex maze honeycombed with calcite formations that continue to change, albeit slowly.

("Unsung Splendor," *Audubon,* July-August, 1996, p.76)

Fair use or plagiarism? The two different worlds of South Dakota's Wind Cave National Park offer a less-visited alternative to Mount Rushmore. The world above ground, an undulating landscape of prairie grass, appears as it must have to the first pioneers who settled here. The world below ground, the cave itself, extends for seventy-eight miles. One of the most ancient of caves, it is covered with elaborate rock forms many millions of years old ("Unsung Splendor" 76).

2. *An original source:* National parks have become plagued by much of the urban frenzy from which people try to flee in the first place. Besides being the home of America's highest mountain, biggest glacier, tallest geyser, and longest cave, the park system now has some of the densest crowds, dirtiest air, ugliest architecture, and longest traffic jams. Last year the national-park system's 367 areas drew 273 million visitors, more than double the crowds of 30 years ago, and the throng is expected to double again in just a decade.

   (David Seideman, "Going Wild," *Time,* July 25, 1994, p. 26)

   Fair use or plagiarism? National parks are coming more and more to resemble places people want to flee. Not only do they contain the United States' highest mountain, biggest glacier, tallest geyser, and longest cave, they also have some of the densest crowds, dirtiest air, ugliest architecture, and longest traffic jams. Today's visitors are more than double the crowds of thirty years ago, and the throngs will double again in just a decade.

3. *An original source:* Overcrowding is affecting even the air above Grand Canyon. All told, 43 different services provide as many as 10,000 plane and helicopter flights over the canyon during peak summer months.

   (Leon Jaroff, "Crunch Time at the Canyon," *Time,* July 3, 1995, p. 76)

   Fair use or plagiarism? Even the skies above Grand Canyon are overcrowded. "All told," reports Leon Jaroff, "43 different services provide as many as 10,000 plane and helicopter flights over the canyon during peak summer months" ("Crunch Time" 46).

Exercise 95--Writing Parenthetical Citations

Write correct and complete parenthetical citations for each of the following situations. Use the appropriate Modern Language Association or American Psychological Association formate style. For the MLA style, see 51b in *The Ready Reference Handbook;* for the APA style, see 54a.

a. You are summarizing a passage from page 824 of William R. Lowry's article "Land of the Fee: Entrance Fees and the National Park Service." It appears in the December 1993 *Political Research Quarterly* (volume 46, number 4), on pages 823-846. You mention Lowry's name and the title of his essay in the text of your research paper. You are using only one work by Lowry. What will you put in your parenthetical citation? Where will you place this citation?

( )

b. You are quoting from a one-page newspaper article by Tom Knudsen, "Sierra's Problem: Too Many People," that appeared in the *Sacramento Bee,* June 11, 1996, page B1. You mention Knudsen's name in the text of your research paper. You are using only one work by Knudsen. What will you put in your parenthetical citation?

( )

1. You are quoting a passage from page 29 of Craig L. Shafer's *Nature Reserves: Island Theory and Conservation Practice* (Smithsonian Institute Press, 1990). Because you are quoting at length, you will present your quotation in block form. You mention Shafer's name in the text of your paper. Later you plan to summarize from a periodical article he has written. What will you put in this first citation of something Shafer has written? Where will you place this citation?

   ( )

2. You are summarizing some facts and figures that appear on page 12 in Donella Meadows' article "The Fall of the Wild," which appeared in *Amicus Journal* (Spring, 1996, pages 12-13). You do not mention Meadows' name or the title of her article in the text of her paper. Later in your paper you intend to quote from another article she has written and published in a different journal. What will you put in this first citation of something Meadows has written?

   ( )

3. You wish to quote nature writer Edward Abbey. You have found his words on page 129 of an essay by Stanley Harbert, "Prairies on Fire," published in an anthology, *This Dying Land,* edited by Sarah Jean Wanzer. You mention Abbey by name in the text of your paper but provide no other information about the source of your quotation. What will you put in your parenthetical citation?

   ( )

Argument and Persuasion

Exercise 96--Writing Arguable Claims

Decide whether each of the following sentences is an arguable claim. If it is arguable as written, write "arguable" after it. If it is not an arguable assertion, write "unarguable" after it. If it is an arguable claim that could be made more exact or specific, revise it. More than one effective revision is possible. To learn to write arguable claims, see 57a in *The Ready Reference Handbook*. Answers to lettered items appear in the back of this booklet. Example:

> **Raise highway speed limits.** *The federal government should raise interstate highway speed limits to seventy-five miles per hour in uncongested areas where the terrain permits.*

a. President Richard M. Nixon was forced to resign the presidency because the US Congress had threatened him with impeachment.

b. The first *Star Wars* movie was the best movie I've ever seen.

c. Eliminate all grades.

d. Addiction to television stifles imaginative thinking.

e. The majority of those Americans receiving welfare assistance are unable to support themselves and unable to become self-supporting.

1. It looks like it might rain tomorrow.
2. In the United States, the death penalty sentences are given unfairly to minorities and the poor.
3. All human beings are created equal.
4. Each year increasing numbers of crimes are committed in American suburbs.
5. Each year American suburbs become increasingly dangerous places in which to live and raise children.

Exercise 97--Identifying Logical Fallacies

Identify the logical fallacies in each of the following brief arguments. There may be more than one fallacy in each argument. To learn to identify fallacies, see 57d in *The Ready Reference Handbook*. Answers to lettered items appear in the back of this booklet. Example:

Those weak-kneed liberal opponents of the death penalty fail to see that their most devoted allies are the animalistic residents of every Death Row in America.

Against the person (ad hominem)

a. Obviously Jenny cannot be lazy, or she wouldn't be the straight-A student she is. Jeff must be the lazy one, because if he had any energy or ambition, he would earn high grades, too.

b. Yes, the Q-80 Sportster's gasoline tank is in the trunk and its bumpers are too thin to withstand a one-mile-per-hour collision. But see that aerodynamic styling? The Q-80 is designed to knife through the air and turn heads. Imagine yourself behind the wheel cruising down the highway, cutting through traffic, that eight-speaker stereo rockin' and rollin'. And look at that paint job! Nighthawk black. Now, if you'll just sign this sales contract right here.

c. It's as plain as can be. Anyone who tries to drive to work in rush-hour traffic is bound to be late. Betty's late. She must be out there on the freeway somewhere.

d. Over the past few years I've failed far more students than I've passed. This year, I'm giving most students in my classes D's and F's. And I see that admissions test scores have gone down again for the fifth straight year. Obviously, today's State U students are not as intelligent as those of former generations.

e. Well, I see the Columbus Clydesdales have lost another basketball game. I'll tell you why--because they're losers, that's why. And losers never win.

1. I'm going to go to the mall this afternoon and buy myself a pair of Thomas Tookas jeans. I saw the President of the United States wearing a pair. And the singers Willie Winsome and Sonja Slade, too. They're the world's largest selling blue jeans. Everybody's wearing them.

2. Look at yourself! If you don't start exercising and eating properly, you're going to be a physical wreck before you're twenty-five.

3. I say abortion is wrong, an evil, bloody rite conducted in homage to the false gods of self-interest and self-gratification. Spend no more than a few minutes in an abortion mill witnessing the destruction of tiny lives by bloody-handed surgeons, seeing their fragile, broken bodies thrown out like yesterday's trash, and you'll agree with me.

4. Sure, you can support welfare payments to the poor. You're a high-living, filthy-rich member of the upper class who probably has a whole battery of high-priced tax lawyers. I'll bet you don't pay a dime in taxes.

5. If you value your job, I encourage you to reconsider before you cast your vote in favor of a union at this company.

6. We citizens are members of what is known as the body politic. If a diseased or infected part of the human body--the appendix, for example--threatens the whole body, it is removed or destroyed. The same should be true of murderers, who threaten the body politic with their

poisonous deeds as surely as a diseased appendix threatens the human body. Like a diseased organ, the murderer should be removed from the body politic and destroyed.

7. The American way is the democratic way, the family-values way, the community morality way. But along comes this artist Melvin Finster with his paintings of ugly, weird-looking naked people, and he expects to display them without anyone's comment in the university art gallery, to be viewed by any over-intellectual, artsy, academic type who wants to look at something corrupt. These paintings deserve to be banned, I say.

8. I see on this applicant's transcript that she started her academic career at a community college instead of a four-year college or university. She must not have been a very good student.

9. Don't worry about travelling abroad and being able to speak only English. You'll do just fine. After all, English is the universal language. Everybody speaks it.

10. Boys do better on math tests than girls, and math is the most difficult subject, so boy's must be smarter than girls.

Answers to Lettered Exercises

Identifying Grammar

Exercise 6--Identifying Nouns

a. Honey, flies, vinegar; b. Wildness, preservation, world; c. Convictions, enemies, truth, lies; d. lies, silence; e. courage, resistance, fear, mastery, fear, absence, fear

Exercise 7--Identifying Pronouns

a. We, itself; b. We, those, who, us, those, whom, we; c. you, something, someone, me; d. that, us, us, we, them; e. everyone, their (pronoun/adjective)

Exercise 8--Identifying Verbs

a. forget, 'll [will] make; b. shrinks, expands; c. applauds, does; d. can be created; e. can be grasped

Exercise 9--Identifying Adjectives and Adverbs

a. Adjectives: A (article), great, a (article), great; b. Adjectives: a (article), blind, an (article); adverbs: even, occasionally; c. Adjective-like verbs: impoverished, isolated; d. Adjectives: Old, bad, the (article); adverb: so; e. Adjective: No; adjective-like verb: depraved; adverbs: ever, suddenly

Exercise 10--Identifying Subjects and Verbs

a. Subject: you; verb: can tell; b. Subject : You [understood]; verb: hitch; c. Subject: Love and a cough; verb: cannot be hid; d. Subject: Dreaming; verb: permits; e. Subject: an easy solution; verb: is

Exercise 11--Identifying Prepositional Phrases

a. of life (adjective phrase modifying *verdict*); b. without a man (adjective phrase modifying *woman*), like a fish (complement), without a bicycle (adjective phrase modifying *fish*); c. in silence (adverb phrase modifying *told*); d. of writing something (adjective phrase modifying *art*), at once (adverb phrase modifying *grasped*); e. of Humor (adjective phrase modifying *source*), in heaven (adverb phrase modifying *is*)

Exercise 12--Identifying Verbals and Verbal Phrases

a. Barking (participle modifying *dogs*); b. to do something (infinitive phrase direct object); c. Concealing (gerund subject of the sentence), to cure it (infinitive phrase modifying *way*); d. to be avoided (infinitive complement), convincing (participle complement); e. tinkering (gerund object of the preposition *of*), to save all the parts (infinitive phrase complement).

Exercise 13--Identifying Dependent Clauses

a. that require new clothes (adjective clause modifying *clothes*); b. because it is quick to hope (adverb clause modifying *deceived*); c. who we are (noun clause direct object of *forget*); d. that there are no golden rules (noun clause complement); e. what has been forgotten (noun clause object of the preposition *except*)

Exercise 14--Identifying Sentence Types

a. simple; b. complex (dependent clause: *Although the world is full of suffering*); c. compound; d. compound-complex (dependent clause: *that almost everything said about it is like to be true*); e. compound-complex (dependent clause: *that's democracy*)

Editing Grammar

Exercise 17--Fixing Fragments

a. The causes of social status are many: the possession of money, education, relationship to political power, the accidents of birth or geography, even physical appearance.
b. Strategies in chess are determined by the designated movements of each piece as well as the initial arrangement of the pieces on the board.
c. Correct
d. The majority of smokers begin to smoke as teenagers, seventy-five percent by age seventeen, eighty-nine percent by age nineteen.
e. Gena lay awake throughout the storm, listening to the branches of the ancient crabapple scratching the side of her house.

Exercise 19--Fixing Comma Splices

a. As we stood at the grave side, we had no words to share with one another. We had only our silent sorrow.
b. I was involved in a serious accident during my sophomore year of high school; ironically, it occurred on the last day of driver's ed.
c. Correct
d. Women and girls have no reason to fear hemophilia, or bleeder's disease; only males are affected.
e. Correct

Exercise 20--Fixing Fused Sentences

a. Pessimists never hope for the best; they always expect the worst.
b. Losing her second job in six months didn't seem to bother Charlene. She took the disappointment with her usual wisecrack and a grin.
c. When they were less than two years old, the Fox children were put in a foster home and grew up knowing nothing of what had happened to their parents.
d. My background is similar to Irene's. My mother is Spanish and came to the U.S. just before I was born.
e. Correct

Exercise 21--Editing Irregular Verbs

a. Joel lamented that he had lost his most prized possession, the wristwatch his father had given him just before he died.
b. On sale this week at the Edgewood Orchard Gallery are the most beautiful scarves, each one woven from natural fibers.
c. When the police saw the thief's footprints leading away from the river, they knew at once where he had hidden the money from the robbery.
d. The minister rose from his seat and led the congregation in the first hymn of the service.
e. The committee has selected its final candidates, interviewed them, evaluated their strengths, and written out its recommendation.

Exercise 22--Editing Verb Tenses

a. We returned home from California by the same route that had taken us there.
b. More movies have been made of *Romeo and Juliet* than any other Shakespeare play.
c. At Matt and Joe's funeral, we laughed as much as we cried, remembering all the good times we had had with them.
d. Correct
e. Throughout the history of the United States, minorities and women have been discriminated against.

Exercise 23--Editing Verb Forms

a. My aunt and uncle have recently retired to a small town in Arkansas charmingly named Mountain Home.
b. Darren used to believe that people on welfare are all lazy bums.
c. We would have been here hours ago if the mechanic had fixed the car the way he was supposed to.
d. Does he have the slightest idea how inconsiderate he is to be doing something else when people are trying to talk to him?
e. Correct

Exercise 24--Choosing the Subjunctive or Indicative Mood

a. Attendance at the final Swirling Ants concert was limited only by the size of the . auditorium.
b. The agent for the Swirling Ants quartet required that the number of concerts be limited to two.
c. If I were you, I would ask that the store owner return your check.
d. We could leave for work on time if everyone in the car pool were punctual.
e. Most gun owners insist that the US Constitution gives them the right to bear arms.

Exercise 25--Editing Subject-Verb Agreement

a. The economic well-being of virtually all of Stratford's 35,000 residents depends upon the success of their annual summer theater festival.
b. In New York City alone there are an estimated 250,000 intravenous drug users at risk of contracting AIDS.
c. New housing developments and the construction of a new highway have forced the area's deer population to forage in people's back yards.
d. Neither Florida nor California has much appeal to warm weather vacationers seeking adventure as well as sunshine.
e. Every one of the hot air balloons was decorated in bright, almost surreal colors.

Exercise 26--Editing Subject-Verb Agreement

a. People who have been laid off or downsized know why economics is referred to as "the dismal science."
b. John Knudsen's paintings and sculpture are varied in technique but always devoted to urban themes.
c. The silence of the brooding, majestic pines and firs creates a somber mood in the park's visitors.
d. In the past several months, there have been several cases of Dengue fever reported in Texas.
e. Commerce Secretary Ron Brown, in addition to his staff and the plane's crew, was killed in the crash.

Exercise 27--Editing Pronoun-Antecedent Agreement

a. When my parents sat me down to tell me of their divorce, I heard their words, but none of them made any sense.
b. Everyone experiences depression at some point in his or her life.
c. Hideaway Resort is widely known for its inexpensive but comfortable and activity-filled vacations.
d. Correct
e. Unable to speak the language and knowing little about local customs, we did what anyone would do for protection from con artists and thieves.

Exercise 28--Editing Pronoun Reference

a. Karen had no desire to taste the goat's milk, and she was certain she didn't want to milk the goat.
b. Betty shared the exciting news about her winning lottery ticket with Adele.
c. Morale at my company is low because employees don't know one another or understand any job besides their own. This situation makes it difficult to increase productivity.
d. Avid readers should stop at the Book Nook for the weekly specials on adult and children's books of all kinds.
e. In today's highly mobile society, a person can easily lose touch with family members who have been forced to relocate as part of their jobs.

Exercise 29--Editing Pronoun Case Forms

a. Correct
b. Janet, Jeffrey, Patricia, and I will be pleased to help with the Oxfam Fund Drive.
c. As my two friends and I were setting up out tents at sunset, we looked up and saw four or five black bears near the edge of the woods.
d. You may not see the difference, but we conscientious objectors call ourselves "draft resisters" not "draft dodgers."
e. I was delighted when Edward gave my husband and me two tickets to the new Tom Stoppard play.

Exercise 30--Choosing **Who** *or* **Whom, Whoever** *or* **Whomever**

a. Three of the people whom the grand jury has identified have long criminal records.
b. In politics today, it's not necessarily the person who shakes the most hands who wins the election.
c. During the holidays, we give clothing and food to whoever needs them the most.
d. Who was nominated for this years best actor award?
e. The people who receive the best medical care are usually the ones who can afford to pay for it.

Exercise 31--Editing Adjectives and Adverbs

a. Correct
b. The man in the clown suit and greasy makeup looked at me peculiarly.
c. Correct
d. Joshua had the happiest of childhoods.
e. On the balance beam, Sharon performed well.

Exercise 32--Editing Faulty Parallelism

a. The campsites in many national parks have electricity and running water.
b. According to a recent Canadian study, the keys to financial success are education, hard work, and the avoidance of risks.

c. Today, many college students use telephones to register for their classes and to reserve seats for special on-campus events.
d. As my father's cancer worsened, he debated whether to end the painful chemotherapy or continue to battle his terrible disease.
e. Erin would rather spend her weekend surfing the Internet on her computer than dancing the night away at a fancy club.

Crafting Sentences

Exercise 33--Using the Active and Passive Voice

a. Igneous rocks are produced by the cooling of molten lava.
b. Enormous pictures of water lilies were painted by the French impressionist Claude Monet.
c. Dinner will be cooked for us by Ben.
d. Roberta is taking karate lessons.
e. Gigantic stellar explosions may release cosmic rays into space.

Exercise 34--Editing the Active and Passive Voice

a. Between 1900 and 1972, more than 150 innocent men were condemned to die by US courts, and at least 23 of them were executed.
b. Genetic engineers have inserted a polyester gene into a cotton plant in order to grow wrinkle-free fibers as warm as wool.
c. Writers of arguments should take care to use only facts and generally accepted truths.
d. Correct [present perfect tense, active voice]
e. Correct [present tense, passive voice]

Exercise 35--Emphasizing with Subordination

a. The greatest decline in cancer death rates has been among African-American men, although their death rates are still higher than those of whites.
b. Stress and depression trigger the release of hormones that may cause brittle bones, infections, and even cancer.
c. On January 30, 1969, the Beatles gave their final live performance, an impromptu set on the roof of their London Apple Corps offices.
d. More than two dozen glaciers flow down the slopes of Mount Rainier, ending at the timberline at an elevation of 6,500 feet.
e. The great Apache war leader Geronimo was actually named Goyathlay, meaning "one who yawns" in Apache.

Exercise 36--Emphasizing with Coordination

a. Barry and Sheri telephoned to say that they were unable to attend this year's community clean-up day, yet two hours later they arrived with rakes, brooms, and garbage bags.
b. Improved urban highways are reducing not only commuter travel times but also accident rates.
c. The evidence indicates that capital punishment does not prevent murders and is disproportionally applied to the poor and minorities; therefore, it should be abolished.

d. Neither strong head winds nor a badly ripped mainsail prevented Jerry Mount and his crew from completing their first race to Mackinaw Island.
e. The Mason-Dixon line is popularly considered the dividing line between the northern and southern states; actually, it marks the border between Pennsylvania on the north and Maryland and West Virginia on the south.

Exercise 37--Emphasizing with Subordination and Coordination

a. Although lightning is usually associated with thunderstorms, it may also be produced by snowstorms, sandstorms, even the clouds over erupting volcanoes.
b. Ball lightning, a spherical flash, varies in size from three to three hundred feet in diameter and lasts less than five seconds.
c. The abominable snowman, also known as the "yeti," is a giant creature that supposedly roams the mountains at night looking for victims.
d. It is described as having an upright posture, a covering of black to reddish hair, and the appearance of a bear, ape, or human.
e. In one version of the story of Lady Godiva, she was observed by only one person, a tailor, the original Peeping Tom, who was struck blind by what he saw.

Exercise 40--Variety: Combining Choppy Sentences

a. Most of us can heavily influence our chances of becoming cancer victims. So concluded the Harvard University School of Public Health in a recent study of the causes of cancer deaths. It identified unhealthy choices as the cause of most of these deaths: smoking causes thirty-five percent; poor diet and obesity, thirty percent; and lack of exercise, five percent. Only a small percentage of cancer deaths is caused by environmental carcinogens, family history, virus, alcohol, and socio-economic status.

Exercise 41--Variety: Dividing Rambling Sentences

a. From the early 19th century to the 1860s, the Oregon Trail was the primary route to the American west. The trail carried thousands of pioneers nearly 2,000 miles from Independence Missouri to the rich farmland of the Willamette Valley in Oregon country, ending at Fort Vancouver, the site of modern Vancouver, Washington.

b. The main route ran west from Independence and then northwest to Fort Kearney. It turned west again along the Platte and North Platte rivers to Fort Laramie, crossing the Rockies by South Pass. From there it veered north to Fort Hall, where it picked up the Snake River flowing to Fort Boise, in what is now Idaho. Finally, it swung northwest to the Columbia River, which the pioneers usually navigated by raft to Fort Vancouver.

Exercise 43--Editing for Varied Sentence Structure

a. Often performing the most menial tasks, more than five million Americans work for the prescribed minimum wage.
b. To assure the basic health and well being of workers was the original purpose of the minimum wage.

c. When they reach the end of the month and bills pile up, many low-wage workers are forced to turn to relatives' charity and government assistance .
d. Within the next ten years, part-time workers will outnumber full-time workers.
e. The nation's major private employer, Manpower Incorporated, is an employment agency providing temporary workers.

Exercise 44--Editing Faulty Predication and Mixed Constructions

a. Removing the hood it makes it possible to lift the engine from the car.
b. Although Darrell Kaminsky is just beginning his professional basketball career, he shows the potential of soon becoming an All-Pro.
c. A number of waste disposal sites have begun to leak and will eventually have to be cleaned up and their contents redumped.
d. Despite what some social critics say, America still exists as kind of melting pot in which we are all thrown to blend into one nation.
e. Back in the 1960s, when my parents were young, the economy seemed very bountiful.

Exercise 45--Editing Faulty Comparisons and Omitted Words

a. After hours of trudging through thick brush and over damp, soggy ground, Eric and Emily finally came upon a small clearing where they could set up their tent.
b. Some people assume that because no one in their family has had cancer, they won't have it either.
c. What I've discovered in my interviews is that children under the age of ten tend to have musical tastes similar to their parents' tastes.
d. There is no better time to observe mob behavior than during professional sporting events.
e. The features of one computer are pretty much the same as those of every other computer in the same price range.

Exercise 46--Editing Mixed and Incomplete Messages

a. The Oklahoma City bombing was one of those tragic incidents which draw a nation's citizens together.
b. At the beginning of the test, the animal is placed in a small device from which only its head protrudes.
c. Next, the animal's lower eyelids are pulled away from the eyes to form a cup into which shampoo is poured.
d. She could only hope the jury would believe her account of the crime more than the prosecuting attorney's account.
e. No one I know admires the courage of the astronauts as much as I do.

Exercise 47--Editing Misplaced Modifiers

a. Albert intended to eat only one chocolate-covered doughnut.
b. As the months passed, dust began to thicken on bookcases, file cabinets, and desks.
c. After paddling our canoes for twelve hours, none of us thought night would ever come.

d. On the walls of the restaurant are large frames containing records and tapes of famous musical artists plated with silver, gold, and platinum.
e. After a lunch break, I was walking back to the courthouse where I was serving on jury duty.

Exercise 48--Editing Dangling Modifiers

a. Chef Edgar has served diners throughout Europe, including royalty.
b. From watching people toss a frisbee around in the park, I think playing with it must be very relaxing.
c. When the championship game is over, we hope the victory flag will be hoisted over our stadium.
d. Life becomes more difficult for most young people after they reach what lawyers call the age of accountability,.
e. Some jobs are not satisfying or glamorous but do pay good wages, working in a supermarket, for instance.

Exercise 49--Editing Faulty Shifts

a. One reason I enjoy rock 'n' roll so much is the joyful release the music offers me.
b. When I wasn't horseback riding or water skiing, the resort staff provided me with many other recreational activities to choose from.
c. Lenore believes that illegal immigrants should be deported and their jobs given to American citizens now receiving welfare payments.
d. Within the last five years, two of Decatur's largest manufacturing plants have shut down, and three others are heavily reducing their staffs.
e. When a stager first begins to mix chemicals into paint, he or she must be careful to mix the correct chemicals in the proper amount.

Choosing Words

Exercise 50--Editing for Exact Words

a. By the end of the third day of the Battle of Gettysburg, the Confederate troops had been entirely defeated.
b. Sunlight filtered into the room through sheer curtains on the patio doors.
c. A lot of people refuse to accept scientific theories based on computer models rather than facts.
d. Of course, capital punishment is intended to deter potentially deviant behavior.
e. Susan joined the local country club searching for prospective clients to buy her insurance policies.

Exercise 52--Editing for Idiomatic Words

a. Creationists offer a novel solution to the extinction of the dinosaurs.
b. For me, cross-country skiing is preferable to down-hill skiing.
c. The mediator instructed the union and management to try to settle their differences in one all-night bargaining session.

d. Everyone tries to discourage me from majoring in journalism.
e. At the end of the State of the Union Address, Cheryl indicated that she differed with the President on several of his tax proposals.

Exercise 55--Editing Clichés and Mixed Metaphors

a. After an incredibly difficult semester of working thirty hours a week and carrying five courses, I'm slowly reorganizing my life.
b. Two term papers due during finals week made me decide that I had to change my life.
c. Clouds of fireflies seemed to race by as our car glided like a cruise missile down the dark, deserted road.
d. Caught up in the intense pressures of a large city like New York, residents have no time to pause and enjoy life's small sensory pleasures.
e. The question of whether to legalize drugs is difficult and multi-sided.

Exercise 56--Editing for Words Appropriate to Academic and Public Writing

a. The years following the stock market crash of 1929 were difficult for almost all Americans.
b. My low aptitude test scores almost denied me admission to college. I was accepted at two state schools, however.
c. The writer Oscar Ramirez explores the way in which American culture interacts with immigrant cultures and is transformed.
d. Cynical politicians profess their support for election finance reform--until they are elected.
e. By installing tape recorders in his White House office, President Nixon made his impeachment and the conviction of his friends possible.

Exercise 57--Editing for Jargon and Pretentious or Misleading Words

a. We regret to inform you that your brother died at 4:13 p.m.
b. Pickleworth's Restaurant offers large portions presented by skilled servers dressed in turn-of-the-century Victorian costumes.
c. To succeed we must organize our tasks in their order of importance.
d. This house must be rebuilt before it can be sold.
e. The 375 inhabitants of the DeVille Hotel were evacuated safely shortly after the beginning of the fire. One elderly man died after leaping in panic from the roof.

Exercise 58--Editing for Sexist and Other Offensive Words

a. When our forebears came to this country, most dreamed of more than economic security.
b. When professional athletes signs their first professional sports contract, they may not know what to do with their instant wealth.
c. In most Western nations, dark-skinned people still do not receive the kind of treatment that light-skinned people do.
d. All humankind, rich and poor alike, will eventually suffer if birth rates are not reduced.
e. Elspeth is so well conditioned and self-disciplined that she's even planning to enter this year's Boston Marathon.

Exercise 59--Editing for Wordiness

a. Some elderly people resist seeing themselves as old.
b. When the Christmas holidays come, I purchase all of my gifts from catalogs.
c. Bide-a-Wee Resort has a wide variety of campsites: pull-through sites with electricity and water, electricity-only sites, and primitive sites carved into bluffs.
d. Many kinds of waste toxins linger in landfills, polluting the soil and ground water for dozens, even hundreds of years.
e. An executive secretary is more an administrative assistant than clerk or typist.

Editing English as a Second Language

Exercise 60--Using Articles

a. Jewelry is my wife's favorite gift.
b. The jewelry she prefers is made of sterling silver.
c. English looks simpler than an inflected language like French.
d. The Korean language resembles Japanese in grammatical structure, but it uses a different writing system known as Hangul.
e. It seems that each culture has a different standard for beauty.

Exercise 61--Editing Articles and Quantifiers

a. After hiking two more miles, we found an easy way down the mountain.
b. Territorial behavior is expressed by humans and animals alike.
c. Finally, soccer is becoming a popular game in the United States.
d. Every Friday evening I go out to eat with several of my friends.
e. Although I'm not a musician, I enjoy music very much, and the music I enjoy most is jazz.

Exercise 62--Editing for Correct Verb Forms

a. By the time I received my flu shot I had already had the flu twice this year.
b. When the hurricane struck, our car was sitting under two huge palm trees.
c. Hasn't anyone ever told you that cigars can be as deadly as cigarettes?
d. When handling HIV patients, you are not supposed to work with your bare hands.
e. We would have loved to attend the party.

Exercise 63--Choosing Verb Forms in Conditional Sentences

a. Whenever I feel a scratchiness in my throat, I know I'm catching a cold.
b. If there were true social equality, workers would receive equal pay for equal work, whatever their gender.
c. I would have been chosen for the job if I had proofread my application more carefully.
d. Barry will leave for the airport when he finishes packing.

e. The defendant would have agreed to plead guilty if the judge had agreed to a sentence of probation.

Exercise 64--Editing Conditional Sentences

a. You would have seen a spectacular meteor shower if you had gone for a walk with us.
b. If I leave my house by 6 o'clock I will arrive at your house by seven.
c. Ho would be a better musician if he spent more time practicing.
d. If Carol were less outspoken, she would offend fewer people.
e. Whenever I am most absorbed by my work, the telephone rings.

Exercise 65--Choosing Infinitives or Gerunds

a. All workers on the site are required to wear hard hats.
b. Teresa was beginning to think that no one was interested in buying her handmade jewelry.
c. Nashunda advised her clients to file a suit and demand a generous settlement.
d. Seldom do I feel like practicing the piano, but my father encourages me to sit down and begin.
e. Bernard walked next door and asked his neighbors to stop playing their stereo so loudly.

Exercise 66--Editing Infinitives and Gerunds

a. My family and I are planning to go to the Grand Canyon next summer.
b. Correct
c. We are looking forward to seeing lions, elephants, and zebras in the wild game parks of Kenya.
d. Correct
e. After the way they embarrassed me, I refuse to speak to them any more.

Exercise 67--Completing Two-Word Verbs

a. Shut off the engine so that we don't run out of gas.
b. I was so angry that I tore up the letter and threw it away .
c. Timothy and Angela left an hour ago; we'll never catch up with them.
d. Please turn in your assignments by Friday afternoon at the latest.
e. When my best friends come home in the evenings, the first thing they do is turn on their stereo and turn up the volume so that all their neighbors can hear them.

Exercise 68--Editing Omissions and Repetitions

a. I know this is true because it has happened to me.
b. In some parts of Saudi Arabia, ten years may pass without rainfall.
c. The Amazon Valley of eastern Ecuador constitutes about half the country's area.
d. There are many orchards and gardens in the Nile River valley.
e. Because all of Nigeria lies within the tropics, there are only two seasons, wet and dry.

Exercise 69--Editing Summarized Questions and Speech

a. An old man sitting next to me on a park bench said that once he had been wealthy and powerful.
b. In my environmental ethics class we spent a whole week debating whether the federal government should act to preserve wetlands.
c. When I called, Natalie told me she was getting dressed and would be ready in fifteen minutes.
d. After the plane had been in the air for an hour, Stephen nervously asked how long it would be before he arrived in Los Angeles?
e. Yesterday, my supervisor asked me whether I would like to attend this year's COMDEX computer convention in Las Vegas.

Exercise 70--Editing **-ing** *and* **-ed** *Adjectives (Participles)*

a. Correct
b. She thought he was the most fascinating person she had ever met.
c. Casey said she was not interested in attending the urban planning lecture.
d. I had just finished eating breakfast when the telephone rang.
e. After the police used riot control gas, the demonstrators were nauseated for several hours.

Exercise 71--Arranging Cumulative Adjectives and Placing Adverbs

a. Some kind of thick yellow slime was oozing rapidly from a pipe into the small stream.
b. Correct
c. Waiters like to see Armand stroll through a restaurant door because he always leaves large tips.
d. When my rich aunt comes to visit, she often brings little gifts to remind us just how rich she is.
e. During the Vietnam War, several devout Buddhist monks burned themselves to death to protest the conflict.

Exercise 72--Editing Prepositions of Place and Time

a. In most American restaurants, smokers and non-smokers are seated in different areas.
b. Correct
c. When Edgar arrived at the airport, he discovered that his plane was three hours late.
d. I meet so many interesting people at work.
e. For four long blocks a suspicious person followed me on the other side of the street.

Punctuating

Exercise 73--Editing End Punctuation

a. Because most of the Earth is covered in a liquid mantle, science writer Dava Sobel says a more appropriate name for our planet would be "Water."
b. Was Thomas Jefferson the first to declare that human beings have the right to "life, liberty, and the pursuit of happiness"?
c. Most Americans believe that the federal government has hidden proof of UFOs from the public (a surprising twenty-percent believe UFOs represent alien life forms).
d. Correct
e. The Japanese fliers began their surprise attack on Pearl Harbor at 7:50 a.m. and concluded their devastating bombardment by 10 a.m.

Exercise 74--Commas: Punctuating Compounds and Introductory Words

a. Correct
b. To detect the presence of drugs, researchers mix blood with genetically engineered antibodies.
c. When cirrus clouds form, they are frequently a sign of changing weather.
d. Jeff's uncle has smoked cigarettes for forty years, so he shouldn't be surprised at his frequent lung ailments.
e. The water in the upper Rhine River comes primarily from the melting snow of the Alps, but downstream, the primary source is winter rain.

Exercise 75--Commas: Punctuating Series, Adjectives, and Modifiers

a. The old grandfather clock struck the hour with a deep, softly echoing chime.
b. Dyslexia, a severe learning disorder, may be caused by brain malfunction or environmental influences.
c. Correct
d. Sharon didn't discover the burglary until she went into her bedroom, where she found her jewelry box open and empty.
e. St. Augustine, Jamestown, and the Plymouth Colony were three of the earliest European settlements in North America.

Exercise 76--Commas: Other Uses

a. The inmates of US prisons tend to be the poor and uneducated, as you might imagine.
b. The wealthy and well educated also commit crimes but, unlike poor criminals, have the resources to avoid conviction and, if convicted, imprisonment.
c. Many English words come from the names of real people, for example, *boycott* and *lynch*.
d. The fabulous golden city of El Dorado was, as historians recognize, a figment of early Spanish explorers' imaginations.
e. "A soft answer turneth away wrath," the Bible reminds us.

Exercise 77--Commas: All Uses

a. Ralph reached for his pocket calculator, which he carried everywhere, and quickly added up the long list of figures.
b. Correct
c. Francis Bacon said, "Some books are to be tasted, others to be swallowed, and some few to be chewed and digested."
d. Des Moines, Iowa, the state capital, was founded in 1843 and originally called Fort Des Moines.
e. Some of the most intricately designed oriental rugs actually come from Kurdistan, a region of northern Iraq and southern Turkey.

Exercise 78--Editing for Missing and Misused Commas

a. Most people associate bagpipes with Scotland, but they originated in Greece and Asia.
b. If the "big bang" theory is correct, the universe is about 10 billion years old.
c. According to the Catholic doctrine of papal infallibility, the Pope is an imperfect human being, but he cannot lead the church into religious error.
d. Air pollution is severe in Albuquerque because the city is located in a broad, shallow valley.
e. To challenge someone in authority who disagrees with me is not easy to do.

Exercise 79--Punctuating with Commas and Semicolons

a. We judge ourselves by what we feel capable of doing, while others judge us by what we have already done.
b. One never notices what has been done; one can only see what remains to be done.
c. Correct
d. Books are good enough in their own way, but they are a mighty bloodless substitute for life.
e. Think before you speak is criticism's motto; speak before you think is creation's.

Exercise 80--Editing Commas and Semicolons

a. People with heart disease are strongly cautioned to control their anger instead of venting their emotions and risking a heart attack.
b. Vince pulled into the gas station for a fill-up, and as he stood at the pump, his eyes fell on the huge dent in his rear fender.
c. Correct
d. According to the Center on Addiction and Substance Abuse, women get drunk more quickly than men, become addicted to drugs more quickly, and develop substance-abuse illnesses more quickly.
e. The old log cabin stood five feet from the ground on a stone foundation, its log steps leading up to an open doorway.

Exercise 81--Punctuating with Commas, Semicolons, and Colons

a. There are only two families in the world, as grandmother used to say: the haves and the have-nots.
b. Pay attention to your enemies, for they are the first to discover your mistakes.
c. All art is autobiographical: the pearl is the oyster's autobiography.
d. Calamities are of two kinds: misfortune to ourselves and good fortune to others.
e. Samuel Johnson offers writers surprising advice: "Read over your compositions, and wherever you meet with a passage that you think is particularly fine, strike it out."

Exercise 82--Editing Commas, Semicolons, and Colons

a. Barbara's allergies make her so sensitive to food that she can eat only one kind: beige food.
b. Some of the most dangerous sports include climbing, cycling, swimming, skiing, and football.
c. Where is it stated in the Constitution that all Americans are guaranteed happiness and a life as comfortable as the next person's?
d. Correct
e. Victims of AIDS suffer a variety of symptoms, such as coughing, shortness of breath, skin lesions that do not heal, seizures, cramps, diarrhea, and memory loss.

Exercise 83--Editing Apostrophes

a. Gresham's Law refers to people's preference for spending overvalued currency and hoarding undervalued currency.
b. Stacy's sister works as a field investigator in the FBI's Dallas office.
c. The summers of '88 and '89 were America's driest since the dust-bowl years of the Great Depression.
d. The children's delighted cries echoed from the playground.
e. The Old Mill Inn's best menu items are fresh catfish, steak, and tacos.

Exercise 84--Punctuating Quotations

a. When the patient awoke, he asked the surgeon, "Did everything go okay?"
b. "The reward of a thing well done," said Ralph Waldo Emerson, "is to have done it."
c. Correct
d. The ancient philosopher Quintilian defined ambition as "the parent of virtue."
e. Are you familiar with Gwendolyn Brooks's poem "We Real Cool"?

Exercise 85--Editing Quotations

a. The beggar asked Jeff whether he had any spare change.
b. "Are these bags yours or his?" the ticket agent asked.
c. The funeral director indicated that cremation was not as expensive as burial.
d. Midwives provide assistance with what is called "natural childbirth," a process involving no anaesthesia or surgery.
e. "All rise," the bailiff called out to the courtroom.

Exercise 86--Editing the Dash, Parentheses, Brackets, the Ellipsis, and the Slash

a. Ernest Wynder identifies the paradoxical goal of modern medicine as helping "people die young as late in life as possible."
b. Correct
c. The aurora australis (the southern lights) glow as brightly and dynamically in the southern hemisphere as the aurora borealis glow in the northern hemisphere.
d. Reducing welfare payments to poor families--without providing funds for job creation, job training, and day care--will do nothing to reduce the number of poor people.
e. The terrain of China rises almost like steps from the lowlands of the east coast to the high mountains of the west.

Mechanics, Spelling, and Formatting

Exercise 87--Editing Capital Letters

a. The small country town where I grew up was so small that its downtown consisted of only a general store and a tiny post office.
b. Zachary Taylor, twelfth president of the United States, died of cholera after serving for less than one year.
c. Many Hispanics would prefer to be referred to as Latinos or Latinas.
d. My aunt and uncle have invited me to live with them if I attend school near their home.
e. This evening's speech on anti-drug legislation will be given by Attorney General Janet Reno.

Exercise 88--Editing Italics/Underlining

a. Willa Cather's most popular novel is probably *My Antonia*.
b. Correct
c. NASA's *Pathfinder* spacecraft is scheduled to land on Mars on July 4, 1997.
d. Correct
e. The first three books of the New Testament--Matthew, Mark, and Luke--are believed to be based on an earlier account of Jesus's life.

Exercise 89--Editing Abbreviations

a. Correct
b. According to Dr. Herman Tyroler, heart disease is no longer an illness primarily afflicting the affluent.
c. Returning from a night reconnaissance following the Battle of Chancellorsville, General Jackson was wounded by some of his own men, who mistook him for the enemy.
d. Correct
e. Correct

Exercise 90--Editing Numbers

a. The most prolific builder of ancient Egyptian temples was probably King Ramses II.
b. A Chia bust of the late Jerry Garcia of the Grateful Dead rock group, already seeded to grow green hair, sells for $21.95.
c. Montana has recently imposed a 75 mph speed limit on its highways.
d. Correct
e. Correct

Exercise 91--Editing Hyphens

a. Correct
b. When a reward was offered for information about the escaped prisoners, the police switchboard was flooded with calls.
c. One problem with modern housing developments is that street layout prevents the formation of genuine neighborhoods.
d. The "either/or" fallacy treats a many-sided issue as if it had only two sides.
e. Seated in front of me at the theater last night was a well-known television actor.

Exercise 92--Editing Spelling

a. When I was young, my father was transferred frequently, and so we moved a lot. That was all right with me because I was able to see the world for free. [doubling consonants, usage]
b. I've been writing poetry since the beginning of my sophomore year of high school. [doubling consonants]
c. A site for the new sports arena has just been chosen. Planning for the new arena was begun a year and a half ago. [homophones, doubling consonants]
d. When I don't make a sale, I don't get paid, and lately I've been losing lots of money. [irregular verb forms]
e. Neither of my roommates will be living with me next semester; basically, we were incompatible. [*i* before *e*, silent *e*, adding *-ly*, unstressed vowel sounds]
f. The foreword to a book will help a responsible, efficient researcher determine weather the book is worth reading. [homophones, unstressed vowel sounds, *i* before *e*]
g. You may not recognize me when you see me because I now weigh less than I did when I graduated from grammar school. It was an exercise program that helped the most, that and staying as far as possible from the campus dining room. [unpronounced consonants, unstressed vowel sounds, confused consonants, doubling consonants]
h. Have I told you about Dr. Alter, a history professor I had last semester? She is definitely the best teacher I've had. [doubling consonants, silent *e*]
i. My step-father grows the best tomatoes I've ever eaten. [forming plurals]
j. In 45 BC the Romans began the practice of adding an extra day to February to harmonize the calendar with the solar year. [unpronounced consonants, unstressed vowel sounds]
k. Cities such as New York and Los Angeles contain many economically healthy immigrant communities. [changing *y* to *i*, adding *-ly*]
l. Overweight consumers shouldn't be deceived by ads promising weight loss without calorie-cutting. [*i* before *e*, unstressed vowel sounds]
m. Michigan and New York are slowly becoming famous for the quality of the wines produced there. [doubling consonants, silent *e*]
n. The weather along the California coast can be very changeable. [homophones, silent *e*]

o. Government lobbyists have prevented the passage of much necessary legislation. [unpronounced consonants, changing *y* to *i*, doubling consonants]

Research (MLA and APA)

Exercise 93--Writing Source Citations (Bibliography)

a. A book.

MLA: Zaslowsky, Dyan. These American Lands: Parks, Wilderness, and the Public Lands. New York: Holt, 1986.

APA: Zaslowsky, D. (1986). These American lands: Parks, wilderness, and the public lands. New York: Holt & Company.

b. A periodical.

MLA: Morgan, J. Mark. "Resources, Recreationists, and Revenues: A Policy Dilemma for Today's State Park Systems." Environmental Ethics 18.3 (Fall 1996): 279-91.

APA: Morgan, J. M. (1996). Resources, recreationists, and revenues: A policy dilemma for today's state park systems. Environmental Ethics, 18 (3), 279-291.

Exercise 94--Avoiding Plagiarism

a. Fair use summary and direct quotation of key words
b. Plagiarism: a summary that quotes key words without using quotation marks

Exercise 95--Writing Parenthetical Citations

a. MLA: (824), placed at the end of the summary before final punctuation; APA: (1993), placed after the author's name or at the end of the summary before final punctuation.
b. MLA: A parenthetical citation is unnecessary because the article is one page long and the author's last name will direct readers to the full citation in the works cited. APA: (1996, June 11, p. B1).

Argument and Persuasion

Exercise 96--Writing Arguable Claims

a. Unarguable, a factual statement
b. A subjective claim that could be made arguable if it were revised as a value judgment claim evaluating one or more features of the movie.
c. A broad claim that could be made arguable if it were revised to identify the needs or benefits associated with the claim.
d. An arguable claim that would more specific if it were revised to say that excessive television watching stifles imaginative thinking. "Addiction" is a vague word.
e. An arguable factual claim

Exercise 97--Identifying Logical Fallacies

a. Either/or, false cause
b. Red herring
c. False cause
d. Hasty generalization
e. Begging the question

Topics

Use the following topics list to help you find ideas for writing exercises in *The Ready Reference Handbook.* Record your observations about these topics or use them to start you thinking about opinions, people, places, events, or things associated with them.

achievement
adolescence
advice
ambition
anger
animals
anxiety
arguments
apologies
appearance
art
automobiles
babies
beauty
betrayal
books/magazines
boredom
bravery
bureaucracy
censorship
city/country
clothing
conformity
conscience
courage/cowardice
compassion
computers
confidence
creativity

crime
cruelty
chance/luck
change
character
death
cheating
childhood
dreams
drugs
education
environment
fame
family
feelings
flattery
games
happiness/unhappiness
health
hypocrisy
ignorance
laughter/humor
laziness/idleness
leisure
mind/intelligence
music
nature
men/women
parents

parting/departures
past/present/future
poverty
prejudice/intolerance
progress
reading/readers
responsibility/duty
personality
rich/poor
procrastination
simplicity
sincerity
thoughts
travel
truth/lies
skill
smoking
virtue
tv/radio/movies
war/peace
weakness/strength
weather
wisdom/folly
words
work
worry
writing/writers
vanity/egotism
youth/age